TRUTHFUL LIVING

What Christianity

TRUTHFUL

Really Teaches

LIVING

about Recovery

BOYD LUTER
AND
KATHY McREYNOLDS

BAKER
A DIVISION OF
Baker Book House Co

© 1994 by Boyd Luter and Kathy McReynolds

Published by Baker Books
a division of Baker Book House Company
P.O. Box 6287, Grand Rapids, MI 49516-6287

**Published in association with the literary agency of
Alive Communications
P.O. Box 49068
Colorado Springs, CO 80949**

Printed in the United States of America

Library of Congress Cataloging-in-Publication Data

Luter, Boyd.
    Truthful living: what Christianity really teaches about recovery / Boyd
Luter and Kathy McReynolds.
       p. cm.
    Includes bibliographical references and indexes.
    ISBN 0-8010-5692-6
    1. Twelve-step programs—Religious aspects—Christianity. 2. Spiritual
life—Christianity. I. McReynolds, Kathy, 1960–. II. Title.
BV4501.2.L865   1994
261.8′3229—dc20   94-29018

Unless otherwise noted, Scripture quotations are from the New American Standard
Bible, © the Lockman Foundation 1960, 1962, 1963, 1968, 1971, 1972, 1973, 1975,
1977.

Scripture quotations identified NIV are from the HOLY BIBLE, NEW
INTERNATIONAL VERSION®. NIV®. Copyright ©1973, 1978, 1984 by
International Bible Society. Used by permission of Zondervan Publishing House. All
rights reserved.

Scripture quotations identified KJV are from the King James Version of the Bible.

To the evangelical church
in the twenty-first century

May the body of Christ
become emotionally whole
without compromising biblical theology

Contents

Preface

IT WAS SEPTEMBER 1992. The fall semester at Biola University was beginning to pick up momentum. I was busy with my studies and Boyd was immersed in his teaching responsibilities. He had just finished the manuscript for his book *Looking Back, Moving On* (NavPress, 1993) in the summer and was still experiencing the "postpartum" blues from the book project. And I was currently writing my own manuscript on the subject of recovery.

Through personal experience and research for my book, I was thoroughly familiar with the basic tenets and practices of the evangelical Recovery Movement. As I studied this popular movement further, I became increasingly disturbed by the direction it was taking. Examining the fruit it produced in the lives of many believers, I began to wonder if recovery was moving outside the realm of biblical orthodoxy.

Then one afternoon I discussed my thoughts and feelings with Boyd. He considered my observations carefully and he too became interested. Immediately, our mutual concern deepened to conviction and moved us into action. First, we co-authored a response article for the *Christian Research Journal* (Spring 1993) on the subject of recovery.

Second, we team-taught a "Theology of Recovery" class at Biola University/Talbot School of Theology in the spring semester, 1993. And, finally, we collaborated on this book. I initially suggested the book idea, Boyd developed its overall framework, and together we worked to bring this project to life.

Even as Jude was very eager to take a certain direction in his writing and then was led by the Lord to pursue another direction (see Jude 3), so we felt the Lord guiding us to coauthor this book. Our lives were moving in opposite directions, but the Lord placed a common burden in our hearts and gave us this special opportunity to express our concerns. Therefore, we sincerely hope that this book is honoring to him and is an encouragement to his church to "search the Scriptures" (Acts 17:11) to test the concepts being presented as beneficial aids to growth and healing.

Heavenly Father, we thank you for bringing hope and healing to every believing heart. You truly are the Lord of Recovery!

Kathy McReynolds

Acknowledgments

WE OWE DEEP DEBTS of appreciation to the following people.

Boyd: My wife, Cathy, who consistently reminds me that theological truth is merely abstract propositions until it is applied to meet personal needs, some of which are profoundly painful and complex.

Kathy: My husband, Mike, who is my best friend. Thank you for your consistent support and encouragement. You were my inspiration throughout this project.

Our first child, Jessica, who was yet unborn when this manuscript was completed. You were my constant companion throughout the writing of this book. It was such a joy to feel your life growing inside of me. But I couldn't wait to finally see you face to face. I love you, Mama.

Boyd and Kathy: The administration of Talbot School of Theology, which allowed the scheduling of a creative team-taught integrative seminar dealing with the "Theology of Recovery" during spring semester, 1993.

Our "Theology of Recovery" students at Biola University and Talbot School of Theology: Watching you—especially the psychology/counseling majors and those with deep doubts about counseling's validity—work through recovery issues from a theological perspective, as well as your growth as believers in

Christ, including significant healing from some overwhelming background issues, was a great privilege!

Dr. John Carter, for his wise insights in both the psychological and theological realms.

Allan Fisher and Kin Millen of Baker Book House, for their
support of this fresh venture in the ongoing task of applying
evangelical theology to the questions and needs of each new
generation.

Introduction

ERIC GREW UP in a balanced Christian home. He was blessed with a father who taught him to think and a mother who encouraged him to feel. His parents were devoted to the Lord and modeled his love in a consistent manner. As a result, Eric developed a close relationship with God at an early age. Being an inquisitive young man, he read many books about his faith and grew both spiritually and intellectually.

Eric's deep commitment to God and his Word naturally led him to attend a Christian university. His faith was very important to him, and he wanted to learn how to integrate his Christian beliefs with his chosen profession. While he was in college, he desired to develop close male friends. So every semester he got involved in a men's Bible study.

In the study group, the men would share their struggles, pray for each other, and encourage one another in God's Word. But something seemed to be missing. Even though the men in the group were sincere and caring, Eric did not feel that his emotional and spiritual needs were being met. He desired more closeness and intimacy.

That particular semester, Eric found the courage to share his feelings with the group. He told them of his need for more intimacy and his desire to be more transparent with them. Much to his surprise, he discovered that the other men longed for this kind of openness, too.

Ben, one of the members of the group, told them that he was being discipled by someone who could help them build the intimacy they desired. His discipler and mentor, Frank, agreed to come and speak to the group if they fulfilled one request. They would have to take the Myers/Briggs Personality Test before he came. Frank would then analyze the members of the group and give them better direction.

With some hesitancy, the group agreed to take the test. Their excitement overruled their mixed feelings when they realized they were going to learn how to go deeper in relationships.

Frank arrived to find open ears and open hearts, an attitude every teacher longs to see in his students. He briefly examined their tests and then set out to teach them how they could break down their emotional barriers and achieve true intimacy.

Frank began his discussion by telling the group that the Christian university they currently attended was pharisaical. The people there were not honest. But they must be honest with their feelings. If they felt a certain way, they must say it. If they felt like cursing, they must do it. This was an essential part of being a real Christian. They were not responsible for the way other people responded to their honest feelings.

He went on to tell them that in order to develop deep, intimate relationships, they must learn to be safe people. Safe people would not judge and condemn. Safe people would permit others to heal and recover from their broken past. Unsafe people, however, would judge and give advice to others. They would not allow them the freedom to express their pain. True growth could only occur with safe people. He also explained to them that the essence of Christianity was the ability to love God and one's neighbor, and that this should be their primary goal.

Then Frank seemed to contradict himself by redefining the gospel message. He warned the men not to spiritualize their problems by running to God for all the answers. Instead, they should seek out other Christians in order to get their needs met. He also said that all people have bad parts. The goal was not to get the bad parts good but the bad parts loved. Initially, the men thought this was a strange way to interpret the gospel. They had never heard it preached like this in church.

In fact, these men were hearing many concepts they had never heard before, and each of them sounded good. This new teaching was like music to their ears. The men were learning about boundaries, projection, codependency, obsessive/compulsive behavior, owning their own feelings, and how to be safe people. Equipped with this new terminology and understanding the true meaning of the gospel, they were now ready to embark on the journey toward deeper intimacy with one another. They were excited about these relational concepts and could not wait to put them into practice in their next group meeting.

The day finally arrived. The men were prepared to share their hearts. Eric was the first to speak. He told the members of the group that they made him feel good. Their response to his statement was not what he expected. The others launched a verbal attack on him: "Stop being codependent!"; "You're not owning your own reality!"; "We're not responsible for your feelings!"

Eric could not believe it. He had thought these were safe people. Instead, his friends were judging and condemning him simply because he did not express his feelings in the right way. This kind of thing had never occurred before they decided to seek true intimacy.

The group experience went steadily downhill. Rather than growing closer, the members began to distrust one another. Judgment, criticism, and closed-mindedness became the prevailing attitudes in the group. Bible reading and prayer were completely removed from their activities. When someone tried to discuss his relationship with the Lord, he was accused of spiritualizing his problems.

Some of the group members did not understand the new terminology and concepts as well as the others. As a result, they would not always express their thoughts and feelings in the prescribed way. Therefore, these men were asked to leave the group because they were considered to be unsafe.

Eric shed many tears over this situation. His relationship with the Lord was hurting; there was now enmity between him and his friends. What he had wanted was intimacy with God and with his companions. What he got was separation. He had sought healing and recovery, but what he had experienced was division and strife. Distraught and bewildered, Eric finally left the group.

Amy was raised in a broken home. She had a miserable relationship with her mother and never knew her biological father. Her third stepfather, who came into the home when she was ten years old, was an alcoholic. He was extremely violent when he drank and took great pleasure in terrorizing the family. Amy tried her best to protect her younger brother and two sisters, but it didn't always work. The whole family bore the brunt of the stepdad's anger.

Amy's teenage years were full of turmoil. She started experimenting with drugs when she was fourteen. She used everything from marijuana to cocaine. At fifteen she began a life of promiscuity, which included many boyfriends and numerous one-night stands. As a result of all the chaos in her life, she barely graduated from high school with a 1.69 G.P.A.

At eighteen Amy moved in with her longtime lover. She got pregnant, had an abortion, and left him shortly thereafter. At twenty-two she married a man who was much like her alcoholic stepfather. The two of them lived on each other's rage. This stormy relationship ended in divorce two years later.

After her divorce, Amy started searching for the meaning of life. She knew something was missing and she longed to fill the empty places in her heart. Even though she kept herself busy with work and people, she often felt lonely. So she began her search for truth by getting involved in the different world religions. She participated in everything from Mormonism to the New Age Movement, but nothing she tried met her needs or satisfied her thirst for meaning.

Finally, at twenty-five, she became a born-again Christian. Her search was over, her soul was satisfied, and her life was changed. Amy knew she had come face to face with the truth.

She loved the Lord Jesus with all of her heart and desired to serve him for the rest of her life. At last she was able to close the door on her turbulent past. She swore never to think about it again.

Two years into her Christian life, Amy began having horrible nightmares about her childhood. She tried to ignore them, but they continued to grow in frequency and intensity. These terrifying dreams of abuse and neglect started to haunt her during the day. She prayed consistently for the Lord to take the thoughts away, but they rarely left her.

Nevertheless, Amy was a faithful and obedient Christian. She read her Bible constantly, prayed diligently, and served the Lord with unrelenting zeal. But the dreams and thoughts persisted. Eventually, she became depressed and suicidal, but no one knew it. She had learned to hide her feelings well.

This young woman was in desperate need of help. She adamantly refused to go to a counselor, however, because she firmly believed that all she needed was the Lord. He would eventually deliver her from Satan's ferocious attacks. In the meantime, she would continue to pray, read her Bible, and minister in the church.

The depression worsened. Her thoughts of suicide increased. Amy started to experience panic attacks and was afraid to leave the house. Deep in her heart, she knew she needed to talk to someone. She had heard of the Recovery Movement and the psychological insight it had to offer, but she had no intention of learning anything about it. She was being taught in church that psychology was of the world and of the devil.

The preceding true stories, while extreme, clearly illustrate the two prevailing attitudes in the evangelical church today concerning counseling and recovery. There are those who embrace recovery principles wholeheartedly without any discretion whatsoever. And there are others who completely reject psychology and scorn its newly developed subdiscipline: recovery. To be sure, there are many believers whose views on recovery fall between these two extreme positions.[1]

Lack of knowledge and confusion about the nature of recovery account for the wide and varied perspectives on the subject. Curiosity, personal need, or concern for a loved one may still motivate many people to search for answers in recovery literature and programs. Thus, the Recovery Movement has gained momentum over recent years and has become a powerful force in the church today.

As this therapeutic movement continues to grow, more and more believers are beginning to ask serious questions about its purpose and legitimacy. What exactly is recovery? Can recovery techniques and principles really help people who are hurting? More importantly, is recovery *biblical?* These are valid questions which deserve thorough, theologically sound answers.

So far, with rare exceptions, only the Christian psychological community has endeavored to answer these queries to any significant extent.[2] To be sure, some prominent church leaders have written books on recovery too. Their intention, however, was not to answer such questions. Instead, they wrote to criticize and condemn the Recovery Movement. In the process, they have failed to fully address the issues that have been raised.

Christian people can have emotional problems. This is one important truth that the Recovery Movement has brought to the attention of the church. Recovery proponents argue that the emotional aspect of human nature has virtually been ignored in the ministry of the orthodox church. Therefore, they have stepped in and attempted to meet the emotional needs of the hurting part of the Christian population. Consequently, the church must own its part in contributing to the overwhelming success of the Recovery Movement.

Although the Recovery Movement has made a number of positive contributions to the church, there is an increasing need to enforce a scriptural "quality control" on this therapeutic crusade. While Christian psychologists have sought, through their writings, to biblically justify recovery, many of the concepts are becoming more and more questionable.

Theologians are not the only ones noting this possible stray from orthodoxy. Several Christian therapists and counselors are now beginning to criticize their colleagues' books and teachings for their lack of theological soundness.

Archibald Hart, well-known author and the dean of Fuller School of Psychology, has pointed out that "a lot of Christian psychology is theologically bankrupt. We haven't struggled with the great themes of the Christian gospel."[3] As many theologians have failed to adequately probe into the concepts of recovery, so popular psychology has frequently fallen short of true, biblical integration.

Bruce Narramore, author and professor at Rosemead School of Psychology, insists that "if the Christian psychology movement is going to make a lasting contribution to the church, we have to write theologically sound books."[4]

While Christian psychologists have sincerely attempted to integrate biblical principles and recovery concepts, the truth of God's Word has often been compromised. The Scriptures have frequently been interpreted through the lens of psychological theories and presuppositions. Not only has the Bible been forced to say what it never intended to say, its authority has been severely undermined. Rather than being the final judge of all truth, the Bible has often been judged on various levels by psychology.

Tim Stafford points out that Paul Meier has said he had no problem integrating his faith and psychiatry. "But when you read Meier's books you find numerous secular concepts with only a window dressing of biblical authority."[5] Stafford also issues this solemn warning to the church concerning the current psychological movement:

> A psychology that has not found biblical roots could be a secularizing force, smuggling non-Christian ideas into the church. It might produce an amoral, unchallenged people, for whom religion is a form of self-congratulation. It might be the guise under which theological liberalism finally conquers orthodoxy: humanity and its "needs" becoming the measure of all things, God being reduced to a source of comfort and inspiration.[6]

20

Despite this timely and penetrating midcourse evaluation from Stafford, we, the authors of this book, believe that the Recovery Movement has offered a significant amount of biblical insight to the body of Christ. It has opened our eyes to the emotional pain many Christians consistently live with and has shown, to a degree, that the Bible does support the idea of recovery. It has met the deep felt needs of many believers in the evangelical church.

Therefore, it is time for theologians and the Christian community as a whole to take the Recovery Movement seriously. It is not a passing fad. Because of widespread domestic abuse and the breakdown of Christian and non-Christian families alike, the Recovery Movement is here to stay.[7]

Thus far, because integration has been done almost totally from the psychological side, the movement has lacked adequate theological controls. The task of the church is not to eliminate recovery programs, but to place biblical boundaries around them and bring the entire movement under the authority of God's Word.

This book is an attempt to do just that. This is our effort to integrate (or interface, by some approaches to integration) recovery principles and biblical truth without compromising divine authority. It is a comprehensive introduction meant to examine the nature of recovery and how it relates to the major doctrines of evangelical systematic theology.[8]

We consider, for instance, how recovery concepts relate to the biblical doctrine of sin. We point out how the Recovery Movement has failed to embrace all of God's truth concerning sinful humanity and, conversely, how it has helped us to further understand human behavior. Then we try to offer a biblical solution to the tensions and conflicts that exist between theology and recovery. Thus, we have developed a "Theology of Recovery."

We have strived to maintain a balanced and biblical approach to this highly controversial subject. Our position encompasses all of God's truth without neglecting the recovery principles we feel are helpful and biblical. This is a unique book in that it is the first full-blown theological treatment of recovery. We believe that it is a necessary book, but it is by no means the final word.

Our earnest prayer is that others will build on our work and further advance our seminal effort. We hope that we have made a valuable contribution to the church by bringing to light the pertinent issues concerning theology and recovery. We also sincerely hope that we have clearly demonstrated that the Bible, when it is properly interpreted, does indeed support many recovery principles.

1

The Delicate Balance
of Truth and Love

As a result, we are no longer to be children, tossed here and there by waves, and carried about by every wind of doctrine, by the trickery of men, by craftiness in deceitful scheming; but speaking the truth in love, we are to grow up in all aspects into Him, who is the head, even Christ, from whom the whole body, being fitted and held together by that which every joint supplies, according to the proper working of each individual part, causes the growth of the body for the building up of itself in love.

The apostle Paul
Ephesians 4:14–16

PICTURE IN YOUR MIND a circus high-wire balancing act. The performance is taking place without a safety net. This is extremely risky stuff! If anything happens to disturb the delicate balance on that high wire, it will probably result in a long hospitalization or a funeral. Thus, whatever has to be done to achieve and keep the proper balance must be done. It's that simple to understand, though admittedly, hardly simple in practice.

The Danger of Losing Your Balance in Recovery

At first glance, it would not seem that a high-wire act and recovery counseling have anything in common. Looking closer, however, we can see that the frequent tragic results of failure in recovery counseling—long-term (often repeated) hospitalizations and even deaths (e.g., from suicides, overdoses, and extreme physical abuse)—are strikingly similar to what happens when there is failure on the high wire and no safety net below.

The loss of crucial balance is what often leads to tragedy in both arenas. In fact, it is only a very small stretch to say that the recovery process is a kind of emotional high-wire act because of the balance required.

The obvious question that arises from this analogy is what is the delicate balance that must be maintained in fostering recovery? The answer is, in essence, the same that the apostle Paul provided in telling his hearers in Ephesus how to move beyond immaturity (4:13) and instability (4:14): Balance truth and love (4:15). That is the way the body of Christ grows and functions the way it should (4:15–16). Thus, it makes sense that healthy growth and functional (versus dysfunctional) living and interpersonal relationships for the various members of the body—individual Christians—must emphasize the same balance.

Though this equation (Truth + Love = Balance in Recovery) is certainly not as simple as 2 + 2 = 4 in practice, it is still worth consideration for its helpfulness in understanding the needed balance in recovery. After all, facing the truth (about ourselves, our painful backgrounds, and our unhealthy relationships) is at the heart of what it is to begin, and continue, in recovery. Also, love is the elusive butterfly of a huge proportion of those with recovery issues. It is also a life-changing, but sweaty-palms choice[1] that must be learned as a basis for healthy relationships.

What happens if this dynamic duo—truth and love—are not paired in the recovery process? As will be seen in the next two sections, the person in recovery will fall off one side of the high wire, or the other, and the results are indeed tragic.

A Tragic Heart Bypass: Truth without Love

A Jell-O mold is another excellent illustration of balance in recovery. Neither the liquid gelatin mixture nor the metal mold can produce the attractive Jell-O salad or dessert by itself.

Truth without love is like a cold metal mold on a plate. It may be shiny and have an interesting shape, but if you tried biting into it, it would be unyielding, to say the least.

Truth to the exclusion of love was the problem of the church at Ephesus in Revelation 2:1–7. Though Christ commended that congregation for their grasp of, and perseverance in, the truth (2:2–3), he still demanded them to repent (2:5) because of their lack of love (2:4). If they did not do so, the consequences were astoundingly severe: The Lord said that he would shut down that church (2:5).[2]

Certainly, truth without love is hardly ever the problem in a program of recovery counseling. It is, however, very frequently where Christians who are strongly critical of recovery—often without much direct knowledge of what they are lambasting—stand. They loudly emphasize the purity of biblical-theological truth, while a virtual vacuum exists on the other side of the balance scales, where love should be found in equal volume.[3]

Truth without love is also the province of doctrinally sound, but emotionally hurting Christians who are locked in denial. Such people often reason (they literally can't bear to feel) that believing biblical truth is supposed to automatically (and instantaneously) "set you free" (John 8:32 KJV) not only *to* eternal life, but *from* all your other background problems and pain. They doggedly cling to that half-truth with one hand, while repressing their internal suffering with the other.[4]

From one vantage point, this emphasis appears to be correct: It defends scriptural truth! However, truth unbalanced by love[5] is a deadly "heart bypass," just as it was the grievous error of the Ephesian church in Revelation 2:4–5. It's not at all likely that the Lord is any more pleased with such imbalance today than he was in the New Testament period.

In seeing this unloving extreme, from which the Lord requires repentance and transformed behavior (Rev. 2:5), the natural tendency would be a pendulum swing reaction in the opposite direction. In this book we will properly emphasize a biblical-theological perspective on recovery. At the same time, though, we will also seek to balance the overall approach with love, both for the Lord of Recovery[6] and for those who are created in his image: human beings,[7] whether or not they are Christians.

At certain points, that attempted balance will take the form of loving truth. At other junctures (notably in application), it will emerge more as truthful love. The bottom line, as will be seen repeatedly, is that balanced, truthful living is not fully possible (for either Christians with recovery issues or more emotionally healthy believers) without the unified teamwork of truth and love.

From what has just been said, it should not be assumed that those who proclaim "the truth, the whole truth, and nothing but the truth" (in the face of what they perceive as unbiblical recovery) are the villains. After all, every truly evangelical organization that we are aware of, whether church or para-church (including counseling clinics), has some required standard of basic biblical-theological belief and corresponding behavior. The reason for that, of course, is that every consistent evangelical would agree that biblical truth is the final authority[8] in faith and practice.

The problem here clearly is not the emphasis on truth, but rather the absence of love. To go back to the Jell-O mold, it is not the metallic mold that is the difficulty; it's that there's no Jell-O inside to be congealed into a tasty delight.

Boundaries Lacking Authority: Love without Truth

Just as the mold without the Jell-O is undesirable, so is the gelatin mixture without the mold. Without the mold (representing the truth), the liquified gelatin mixture (representing love) has a pleasant taste but no shape. If you accidentally poured it out on a table, counter, or floor, it would spread out far beyond the normal boundaries that would be set by a mold.

The imbalance of leaders and counselors in the recovery movement is often this: to helpfully emphasize the various important aspects of love, but, for one reason or another, to virtually ignore the extensive truth about spiritual recovery in God's written Word. When that happens, there are few, if any, objective boundaries shaping the Christian belief and therapeutic methodology of those in the movement.

This is highly ironic. Without question, the concept of boundaries (i.e., knowing where your personality and responsibility stop and those of others start) is a central part of the standard recovery framework and vocabulary. John Townsend of the Minirth-Meier West Clinic goes so far as to say, "Next to bonding deficits, the problem of unclear boundaries is probably the most serious cause of emotional and spiritual struggles experienced by Christians today."[9] Interestingly, Townsend also asserts that boundaries are "essential for us to be able to love."[10] If Townsend is correct, that would seem to mean that it is very difficult, if not practically impossible, to love properly without boundaries.

The situation is parallel with theological boundaries. Without knowing where the truth of Christian theology stops and secular (or even New Age) approaches to recovery start, there is no way to gauge whether the love a recovery program is fostering is in line with what God commands in the Bible, or an out-of-bounds (i.e., boundaries) counterfeit.

This is a frightening prospect! Since the use of recovery therapy in evangelical counseling is still fairly new, it is highly doubtful that the level of integration needed between that theory/methodology and biblical theology has taken place in many quarters. In certain instances, this theological lack—or, at least, lag time—has been explained in terms of a sort of syllogism of compassionate pragmatism: Many people, including Christians, are hurting; recovery therapy works in healing such pain; so, just do it to help alleviate their pain.

If this new therapy were in the medication-pharmaceutical field, it would still be classified as an experimental drug. If it were in the realm of physical treatment or surgery, it would likely still be considered an experimental procedure. Why? Because, in those fields, there must be extensive long-term testing by the authoritative agency to verify the validity, usefulness, and safety of a medication or form of treatment.

So, what is the bottom-line authority in validating the content and methodology of recovery treatment by evangelical counselors? Is it some kind of "seal of approval" from the American Psychological Association (APA)? How about the endorsement of the Christian Association of Psychological Studies (CAPS)?

The difference between a counselor that just happens to be a professing Christian and a consistent evangelical Christian counselor is that, for the latter, the foundational authority and the last (i.e., Supreme Court–level) word is always God's, in his Word. Scriptural truth is not mere afterthought or window dressing, for what are, at the core, inherently secular psychological concepts and practices.

If these statements seem unduly harsh, or like something someone who doesn't understand the psychological field might say, hear the somber recent evaluation of Archibald Hart, the respected Dean of the School of Psychology at Fuller Theological Seminary:

> Many well-meaning psychologists and psychiatrists who profess Christianity have merely uncritically borrowed the theories and techniques of secular psychology. Professing faith in Christ does not immunize us against distortions.[11]

Suffice it to say that it is just as easy to fall off the high wire of recovery on the side of emphasizing love without a corresponding balance of what could be accurately called "the whole truth, so help me, God," meaning, of course, God-breathed Scripture (2 Tim. 3:16). Love without the boundaries provided by biblical theology can be as misguided as a well-intentioned driver who turns the wrong way on a one-way street.

Herein lies a dose of reality (another primary recovery concept): Thinking you know what you're doing is little help when you're out-of-bounds and headed for a crash! It's a tad late at that point to start asking, "Where did I make a wrong turn?"

Before the evangelical Recovery Movement makes a seriously wrong turn by sporadic proof-texting or squeezing biblical verses into an uncritical psychological framework, those involved are strongly advised to carefully set their biblical-theological boundaries, then maintain them with constant vigilance. Even if they do not succeed in gaining the support of the entire evangelical community in doing so—obviously, you can't please everyone—that will go a long way in earning the respect of that mass of conservative Christians whose constant touchstone is Scripture and scriptural theology.

We don't see any legitimate reason why theological truth and recovery-enhanced love (and those who work in both realms) can't team up and get the job done even better than either focus could separately. Truth and love *must* go together.

Foundational Truth Supporting a Loving Edifice

The apostle Paul's counsel that truth and love produce growth (Eph. 4:15) should also be understood against its natural wider context, the Ephesian epistle. Considering the overall flow of Paul's letter minimizes the possibility that the meaning of a particular verse or idea will be lifted like a slice of pie without proper consideration of its origin/background (factors which, within wise boundaries, are helpful parallels in recovery counseling).

Ephesians consists of three initial chapters of primarily theological content and three completing chapters of largely applicatory material. The tethering "therefore" in 4:1[12] cuts both ways: It means that the behavioral material in Ephesians 4–6 is built upon the foundation of the theology in chapters 1–3; and it also means that the theology expressed in Ephesians 1–3 is not truly complete until it is worked out in behavioral transformation (Eph. 4–6).

This structural balance has important implications for recovery theory and therapy: (1) attitudinal/behavioral transformation, which is the goal sought by recovery, is also the designed outworking of theology; and (2) proceeding to the behavioral without adequately considering the bedrock theology that is involved is short-sighted, virtually setting up a resounding future collapse.

Is it possible this is making too much out of the structure of one of Paul's epistles? Such might be the case if parallel structuring were not also readily apparent in Colossians and Romans and if the background of those two letters were not clearly suggestive of the same points.

Paul writes Colossians to a group of Christians that, for the most part, he had never met face-to-face (Col. 2:1). However, the geographic proximity of Colossae to Ephesus makes it almost certain that the church in Colossae had learned a great deal of Pauline theology during the more than two years the apostle taught daily in Ephesus (Acts 19:8–10).[13] That previous theological exposure largely explains why Colossians is, like Ephesians, structured half theology (Col. 1–2) and half application (Col. 3–4).

The proportion of theology to behavior changes dramatically with Romans, however. About two-thirds of this majestic epistle (Rom. 1–11) is primarily theological, with less than a third behavioral (Rom. 12–15) and the final chapter essentially an extended list of greetings.

To account for the shift in proportion, we do not necessarily need to look any further than the fact Paul had never visited the church at Rome (Rom. 1:10, 13). Nor had the church had the advantage of in-depth previous exposure to Paul's theological teaching.[14] Thus, the apostle takes nothing for granted and painstakingly develops the foundational theological truth before moving to behavioral transformation.

Some have misconstrued the high proportion of theology in Romans in an intellectualizing way, but such an approach is not valid. Four chapters of Romans are rigorously applicational/behavioral in content (Rom. 12–15), much more than either Ephesians or Colossians. Therefore, a proper appraisal is that Romans is no less behavioral than its comparably structured letters. Rather, it is more aware of the need to build a solid theological foundation for behavior when the readers do not have as strong a theological background.

What's the bottom line here for recovery? It would seem that not only is theology foundational to the behavioral treatment needed for recovery, but those believers who are less theologically astute and entering recovery therapy have a greater need for a strong theological base to build upon.

Loving Unity: Choosing to Mature in Belief and Behavior

Sometimes biblical passages make their main point through subtle but elegant literary techniques, instead of baseball-bat-between-the-eyes direct statements. This seems to be the case with Ephesians 4:1–16. This passage employs bracketing (literary bookends) to emphasize the need for, and means of, achieving not just unity, but a *loving* unity. The focus on unity is present from the beginning of the passage to the end. References to the unity of the Spirit (Eph. 4:3) and the unity of the faith (v. 13) stand out readily, as do the "one . . . one . . . one . . ." section (vv. 4–6) and the analogy of the body of Christ (vv. 13, 15–16), which implies unity in diversity (v. 16).

In contrast, the love factor is seen only at the beginning and the end (Eph. 4:2, 15–16). That does not mean it is any less important than unity, however. If anything, its placement as bookends in this key passage strongly implies that love must color all attempts at the kind of unity Paul is calling for.

Let's probe a little further to see the beautiful balance involved. In Ephesians 4:2–3, properly preserving the already-existing basic unity of the Spirit (v. 3) among Christians requires loving behavior (v. 2). This is vitally important. But this behavior is essentially maintenance ("preserve," v. 3), not growth. The growth, and thus recovery-related, aspect is the unity of the faith (v. 13). This higher unity can only come about as all believers (v. 12) gain knowledge (biblical-theological truth) and, correspondingly, grow behaviorally to spiritual maturity (v. 13).

The bookends' positioning of love comes into play here most strikingly. Such growth to maturity together in the faith not only requires the consistent refueling, so to speak, with knowledge/truth (v. 13), it also necessitates dealing with that truth in love (vv. 15–16).

Again the point is made: Spiritual growth, including the more specialized kind that is biblical recovery, cannot take place through either love or truth by itself. It must take place through both love *and* truth, especially if the unity that is to characterize the relationships between Christians as the body of Christ is to be evident.

Balanced Significance: God's Gracious Provision for Biblical Recovery

It should not, however, be assumed that Paul's emphasis on unity in spiritual growth in Ephesians 4:1–16 expects some sort of monolithic sameness as a goal or indication of such unity. This might be the mistaken conclusion of some with recovery issues who have a long-standing tendency to blend in as harmoniously as possible with the relational dynamics around them. But almost exactly the opposite is the case.

Before the dust has had a chance to settle from the discussion of unity and oneness in Ephesians 4:3–6, the apostle brings up diversity (vv. 7–10). He also discusses the establishment of what brings about the balance of unity in diversity in a way that identifies with the biblical recovery process. For the first time grace is brought into the mix (v. 7) in relation to what is normally called spiritual gifts (v. 11).[15]

In an amazing affirmation of God's intention for individual distinctiveness, Paul affirms that Christ has personally apportioned (or tailored) giftedness in each one of us (v. 7). We might be quite satisfied—even totally elated—just to know that we matter enough to the Lord Jesus for him to bestow on us such wonderful spiritual gifts. After all, this reality provides a strong basis for a sense of significance: As a believer, I can know that I am a *gifted* person in a very true sense of the word.

But Paul does not stop with a bare declaration of the giftedness of Christians (Eph. 4:7). He goes on to describe how Christ came to the point of bestowing spiritual gifts, and he does so with a description that is unique in the New Testament. Initially he paraphrases Psalm 68:18 to portray Christ's victory in the resurrection and ascension to heaven (Eph. 4:8, 10) as a parade or processional of a victorious military general. This sets up the spiritual gifts as the spoils of victory Christ generously shares with his people (v. 8).

The most intriguing and relevant part of this discussion of the bestowing of spiritual gifts for recovery is the seemingly parenthetical explanation of what preceded Christ's ascending—his descending (vv. 9–10). For our purposes here, it is not crucial to determine whether descending to "the lower parts of the earth" (v. 9) means Christ's incarnation (i.e., descending from the heavenly realm to earth) or the place of the dead (i.e., the ancient creedal wording that Christ "descended into Hell").[16] Rather, it is Paul's inclusion of the process of descending and ascending that stands out and offers hope.

In whatever way descending may be viewed, it represents the Lord at a low point that had to be overcome. This overcoming—a common term utilized to refer to Christian recovery—took place through the sequential process of the cross, resurrection, and ascension. While there is no further basis in this passage for comparing the nature of overcoming in the recovery process with Christ's victory, it is encouraging to know that the very presence of spiritual gifts in believers' lives is due to the fact the resurrected Lord was the first, and foremost, overcomer.

Establishing Balance and Encouraging Growth

Some of the spiritual gifts in Ephesians 4:7–8 are listed in verse 11. The first two categories ("apostles" and "prophets") are absolutely foundational to the church (Eph. 2:20). Of particular interest to our discussion, however, are the last two: "pastors and teachers" (v. 11).

The term "pastors" literally means "shepherds." It implies the kind of care and concern a good shepherd (John 10:11, 14) demonstrates toward his sheep. This personal touch side of ministry is closely linked with teaching (v. 11),[17] the imparting of the truth of Scripture so Christians might be equipped adequately for ministry (Eph. 4:12; 2 Tim. 3:16–17) and grow to corporate spiritual maturity (Eph. 4:13).

While there are numerous challenging facets to pastoral ministry, a sensitive shepherd must never overlook those sheep who are hurting over and beyond the typical growing pains of the Christian life. This requires at least some basic familiarity not only with recovery issues, but also with the kind of treatment that is available locally or elsewhere.[18]

Sending a hurting person away without providing help may have more to do with ignorance or lack of training than with a lack of basic biblical compassion. Because such cases are not uncommon, there needs to be a retooling of both basic seminary pastoral preparation classwork and continuing education courses offered, as well as other means, to get pastors up to speed in this increasingly needy area of ministry.

As we continue through the 1990s, it will likely become more necessary for pastors to do some hands-on basic recovery counseling. If for no other reasons than limited personal resources and tighter insurance restrictions, pastoral personnel will have to get involved with long-buried emotional upheavals. If they choose not to (and try to ignore the mushrooming internal pain around them), they will not be markedly different from the irresponsible "Go in peace, be warmed and be filled" of James 2:16.

What is needed is a distinctive hybrid of pastoral/theological and specific recovery counseling training. This would implement, at the training level, the crucial balance of truth and love. This would also help church personnel understand much more about the nature, biblical validity, and effectiveness of the para-church Christian counseling organizations to which they might make referrals.

At present, two of the biggest problems between churches and free-standing counseling clinics and ministries are a lack of trust by the church and a lack of accountability to the church by the counselors. Both are largely due to a lack of specific shared knowledge in this area of counseling and a common-ground theological framework for interaction. Both could be squared by offering the kind of reconfigured, integrative pastoral counseling training suggested above.

Balanced Interdependency: The Key to Long-Term Biblical Recovery

In the face of these emerging needs, evangelicals must begin to see themselves not as "us" and "them," but as a team. It is tragic for Christians to break down into groupings of the judgmentally healthy and the emotional lepers. It is pridefully shortsighted, if not self-defeating, for the pastors and counselors who should be helping (both in therapeutic insight and in overriding such simplistic stigmas) to be holding each other at arm's length. The result is a sadly imbalanced independence—unhealthy, uneasy, and distanced.

The biblical fact of the matter is *we all need each other!* This is not the kind of unhealthy need that characterizes codependent relational webs. It is the healthy kind of interdependence that Paul develops in Ephesians 4:12–13, 15–16, that fosters both individual and corporate growth among believers. It is in the matrix of these healthy interdependent relationships that the delicate high-wire balancing act of truth and love can flourish (vv. 15–16). In this context, a wider safety net can be spread, if the body of Christ seriously considers both factors in the truth and love equation.

We believe that such a balanced collective biblical recovery lifestyle is, in fact, possible for the evangelical church. By following the apostle Paul's wise counsel in Ephesians 4:1–16, it *is* do-able for the wider body to walk worthy on the high wire of its Christian calling. What remains is the choice to do it—to walk *together* through the confusing terrain of recovery issues, helping each other balance biblical-theological truth and compassionate love. This is a balancing act that will play to standing-room-only crowds at every turn because it is of supernatural design: a loving lifestyle, full of God's truth (Eph. 4:15).

2

The Authoritative Handbook for Recovery

In pleading for a greater integration of our psychological and spiritual selves I am in no way asserting that psychology is the superior way of knowing the self nor is it to be the supreme judge of truth. If anything, psychology has to be scrutinized by the standards of Scripture, not the other way around.

Archibald Hart
Me, Myself, & I

DID YOU EVER try to assemble even a fairly simple toy without the directions? There are very few sure things in life, but it is a pretty safe bet that before you were finished you had put at least one part in the wrong place or left something out altogether.

When All Else Fails, Read the Directions

No matter how intelligent you are and how much confidence you have in your ability, the directions enclosed by the manufacturer are there for a very good reason: to ensure the correct assembly of the item. So, if you want to make sure you get it right, don't take the risk of trying to figure it all out on your own.

Instead, on the front end of the assembling process, pay close attention to the provided guidelines, instead of waiting until the frustration, even embarrassment, sets in as you realize that something went wrong. At that point, you usually have to take your intended masterpiece apart and reassemble it in line with the directions you should have followed in the first place. This requires some real maturity, because often pride and anger flare up and endanger your finishing the humbling task of reassembly.

This illustration has considerable relevance for the relationship between recovery and theology. When the dust of heated debate settles, the biblical-theological truth provided in Scripture ultimately provides the "manufacturer's instructions," even on a psychological subject like recovery. Those guidelines must be adhered to if the finished product (here, the recovery process) is to function as the manufacturer, God, intended.

Christian psychologist Archibald Hart appears to be relatively close to this perspective when he wrote recently, "Even while providing valuable insights into how the self operates, psychological understanding will always be limited. . . . Our minds need divine revelation to fill in the gaps."[1] Such an outlook by a leader of Hart's stature opens the door for highly constructive dialogue between evangelical psychologists and theologians.

All Truth Is God's Truth, But . . .

By this point, many who work in psychology will have already invoked the verity that all truth is God's truth. This statement has frequently played the role of border patrol along the uneasy boundary between psychology and theology. Whenever those on the psychological side of the aisle have perceived the encroachment of theologians into their territory they have quickly raised the "All truth . . ." banner.

The good news is that this outlook is actually well-suited to mediation between the two disciplines and can contribute greatly to healing the breach between the two arenas. Let's consider how such a truce might be arranged between the two disciplines.

First, we must consider the nature of the truth in each area. Although both psychology and theology are on a similar quest for truth, they pursue it in different settings. Psychology relies mainly on *empirical* methodology (i.e., observing experiments and experience) for its data and conclusions, while theology deals mainly with the *propositional* truth taught in Scripture (John 17:17), approaching it by means of inductive and deductive reasoning. Through these different avenues, both fields have discovered vitally important points and common underlying principles that offer a basis for integration.[2]

But what happens when the findings of evangelical psychologists and orthodox biblical theology are at odds? Hart's considered opinion is to ". . . put psychology in its rightful place: subservient to the revealed word of Scripture,"[3] a statement that echoes the view of the evangelical church throughout its history.[4] Such a perspective does not mean that theologians hold a superior position to psychologists or even that theological methodology is better than that in the psychological realm. It simply recognizes, as consistent evangelicals always have, that the Bible is the final authority in matters where differences exist.

Some may argue that Scripture and theology are not one and the same and that theologians are as capable of making mistakes as psychologists. Attempting to use such an argument represents a kind of double standard. At one level or another, every evangelical psychologist has already tacitly recognized the final authority of biblically-based theology. Whether in the workplace or in the church, each one has agreed to some detailed doctrinal formulation as a binding representation of biblical truth and, in effect, the bottom-line authority in matters of faith and practice. To argue that the very theological base they claim to stand upon and give allegiance to has no right to validate psychological research and therapeutic methodology, areas which certainly relate in one way or another to faith and practice, is borderline hypocrisy at best.

The other alternative is much more dangerous, however. What if certain professing evangelical psychologists/counselors were to come forward and admit that they held no specific theological position, but were committed to some sort of free-floating, undefined "biblical authority" alone? Some unthinking people might momentarily accept such a declaration, but soon would have to ask what that person believes specifically on anything encompassing the quoting of more than one verse of Scripture, a question that requires a correlated theological response. Those of this persuasion could not credibly serve in a school, ministry, or clinic requiring adherence to a certain doctrinal position (as every responsible evangelical organization that we are aware of does). And even if they started their own counseling center, they would be unable to field most of the questions from potential clients, pastors, and other evangelical consumers who have both the right and responsibility to inquire in detail about a therapist's belief structure.

For psychologists, theology can provide the element of Christian quality control that, sooner or later, regulates every successful field where there is potential for abuse, and can also positively validate the professed theological orthodoxy of psychological practitioners. For theologians, consideration of psychological concepts and procedures forces theology to be more and more an applied (and realistic) field.[5] It also challenges the theologian to a necessary contextualization[6] of biblical-theological truth in light of those cutting edge questions and issues in our present society.

With this type of complementary yoking, the grumbling about theological watchdogs by psychologists and psychological mavericks by theologians can be largely laid to rest. The search for all of God's truth can continue unabated.

Figure 2.1 shows how a balanced perspective might be worked out by those with an evangelical commitment to Scripture in the fields of psychology and counseling.

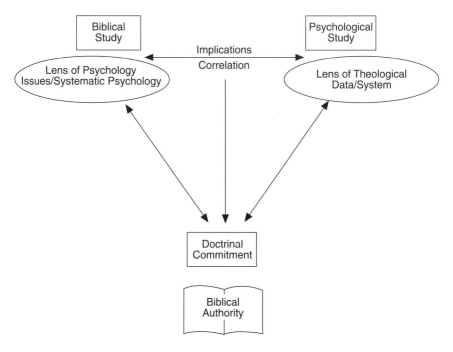

Fig. 2.1

**Checks and Balances for Evangelical Psychologists
Handling Biblical-Theological Truth**

General Revelation and General Recovery

General revelation is that aspect of bibliology that makes it clear that all people are responsible for understanding certain basic truths about God's existence as Creator[7] (Ps. 19:1–6; Rom. 1:19–20). By looking at the beautiful and orderly creation around them or the presence of a conscience within them (Rom. 2:14–15), such people, though far from the Lord in unbelief (Rom. 1:18), can still readily discern such points as God's "invisible attributes . . . eternal power and divine nature" (Rom. 1:20). Yet, even though this general revelation in the wider creation and human nature is sufficient to leave mankind without excuse before God (v. 20), it is insufficient to reconcile humanity with the Creator. The picture of God is in view, but it needs fine-tuning to be clear enough to impart the needed life-transforming information.

From the vantage point of salvation, general revelation represents a significant step in the right direction. However, it is incomplete and inadequate to bring about the necessary final result. While it evokes awareness of God, it cannot save anyone in the fullest sense of the word.

This is where special revelation comes into play, that information about the Lord that can *only* be learned from the revelation of God in Scripture. Special revelation fills in the sizeable gaps left in the framework of general revelation so that the gospel message of justification by grace through faith in the Lord Jesus can adequately be comprehended (Rom. 1–3).

This process and its outcome hauntingly parallel the recovery popularized in the Twelve Step programs.[8] A feature article in *Christianity Today* accurately referred to the limited Christian content of the Twelve Steps (particularly in regard to who God is and the specifics of the gospel message) as "The Hidden Gospel of the 12 Steps."[9] It describes the Christian background and perspective of those who developed the original Twelve Step program, and how the content was generalized to make it acceptable to the widest possible audience.[10]

This generalized recovery approach of the Twelve Steps is a bittersweet two-edged sword. On the one hand, it has persuaded many whose lives were destroyed by alcohol (and other addictions) to take the necessary responsibility for their lives and recovery. On the other hand, it comes no closer to introducing them to the one true God or Jesus Christ than such vague wording as "power greater than ourselves" and "God as we understood him."

For the responsible beginning of general recovery in the lives of a vast multitude of hurting people, we should be very thankful. After all, God in his common grace mercifully "sends rain on the righteous and the unrighteous" (Matt. 5:45). However, altering the short-term direction of tragic lives and providing an awareness that there is a higher power over the universe still stops far short of changing someone's eternal destiny and beginning the transformation process of biblical sanctification.

If the recovery approach began as scriptural Christian concepts (and there is overwhelming evidence that it did) and if recovery counselors really care about those they work with (and we have no doubt that most do), then this short-circuiting of the biblical gospel loses more than it gains over the long haul. In light of the eternal destiny of such people, standard recovery programs are simply a short-term fix.

There is no ultimate reason why such programs, manned by Christians, should not be willing to go far enough scripturally and theologically to bring such lost sheep into the fold of eternal life and the resulting empowerment for inner and behavioral transformation provided by the Holy Spirit.[11] To do otherwise is, in essence, to lead those who are obviously emotionally and spiritually thirsty up to the edge of the water but not let them drink.

As gracious as it is, general revelation saves no one; it simply makes them aware that God exists and holds them responsible for their actions and unbelief. As compassionate as it might be, general recovery also provides no one with eternal life. To begin the full-scale recovery the Lord offers, these baby steps are not enough. The giant steps of the gospel are needed.

Scripture as Inspiration for Recovery

The central biblical passage on the inspiration[12] of the Bible (its ultimate divine origin and infallibility) is 2 Timothy 3:16–17. It also proves to be one of the most important passages on why Scripture was given by the Lord: its practical profitability in transforming our lives. This is the point at which the concept of biblical inspiration links up with recovery.

The profit factor first has to do with teaching (v. 16). This word (Gk. *didaskalia*) is speaking of biblical content being presented in an orderly form. Two related implications should be noted. Such teaching certainly includes a considerable element of doctrinal (theological) instruction, even if it is not the whole focus. And what is received from biblical-theological teaching is the foundation for the other practical steps that follow in 2 Timothy 3:16–17. In other words, biblical-theological teaching is the divinely intended first step on the path to behavioral transformation. To overlook the doctrinal aspect of even profoundly behavioral issues is to overturn the launching pad role God designed scriptural content to play in spiritual growth and emotional healing.

It should not be assumed, however, that the theological profit of God-breathed Scripture (2 Tim. 3:16) is an end in itself. This impression has certainly been left on many occasions in the history of the church by the host of abstract creeds and other doctrinal formulations addressing belief structure but not corresponding attitudes and behavior. The linking sequence in 2 Timothy 3:16–17 demonstrates that theology without lifestyle impact is as much an abortion of the divine intention as attempted behavioral change without an adequate theological base is a bypass of divinely provided truth.

In looking further at God's motive in giving us biblical truth we note that every other part of the process is directly related to recovery. Reproof and correction (2 Tim. 3:16) certainly deal with showing where a person's attitudinal/action patterns have been distorted and dysfunctional (often sinfully)[13] and what must take place for new healthy outlooks and behavior to replace the old ways. Admittedly, what is required for these changes to truly come about may vary greatly from person to person. For a reasonably emotionally healthy person with a smaller issue as the focus of the reproof, the choice to change (and repent when necessary) might be instantaneous. However, for a person with long-standing (often denied and internally buried) problems or sinful patterns, such a monumental midcourse correction may be a fairly lengthy and highly painful process. In this regard, the term usually translated "correction" (Gk. *epanorthōsis*) also has the nuance of "restoration,"[14] implying that the process of correction may be considerably more open-ended timewise than is usually assumed.

"Training in righteousness" (v. 16) definitely fits readily into a biblical recovery framework. Other usage of the idea of training (Gk. *paideia*) has the color of upbringing or parental discipline,[15] in the sense of child-training. This is an accurate description of what must happen when a believer with remaining childish patterns in his or her life begins to come to grips with his or her resistant immaturity. The Scriptures are designed by the Lord to play a kind of parental guidance role in providing insight, healthy disciplinary standards, and other factors needed to grow in righteousness.

The end result of the biblical-theologically based recovery process in 2 Timothy 3:16 is adequacy in those appropriate roles and relationships with future involvement (v. 17). This does not mean that an internal feeling of inadequacy cannot be overcome until one is well down the road of training in righteousness. A proper biblical sense of adequacy in who you are is related to self-image as a child of God made in his image.[16] It does mean, however, that a growing reality of behavioral/relational adequacy is a large part of the joyful outworking of what God expects to take place when biblical-theological truth is allowed to pierce into the deep and sometimes dark recesses of the believer's thoughts and emotions. What an inspiring motivation for pursuing biblical recovery!

Scripture as Inspiration for Recovery Counselors

Like red lights punctuating the flow of traffic in a congested drive to work, chapter divisions in the Bible sometimes occur at very inopportune points in the flow of thought. For all their usefulness as scriptural reference points, these divisions can often leave the false impression of a disconnection between the material in back-to-back chapters.

This is true of the break between 2 Timothy 3:17 and 4:1. It is highly misleading to leave the impression that the inspiration of the Bible is only supposed to have an individualistic internal impact (2 Tim. 3:16–17). Yet such an implication can certainly be drawn by slamming on the brakes at the artificial stop sign after verse 17. By continuing into 2 Timothy 4, however, the wider applicational force of Scripture's inspiration is seen. And, interestingly, this wider arena and impact is closely tied to what is involved in biblical recovery.

In this context (2 Tim. 3:16–17), the solemn charge of verse 1 in chapter 4 provides a more personal sense of accountability and the long-term consequences of actions—both key recovery principles—than did 2 Timothy 3:16. It also means that the recovery process developed in verses 16–17 was conceived by the Lord as much as a preface to helping others (2 Tim. 4:1–4) as for healing oneself.

The trigger command at the beginning of 2 Timothy 4:2 leaves the initial impression that what follows is strictly limited to corporate preaching. However, the related functions and qualities stated in the rest of the verse make it likely that "preach" functions as a herald[17] under authority (v. 1). The wording "reprove, rebuke, exhort, with great patience and instruction" in 2 Timothy 4:2, as well as the portrayal of denial in verses 3–4, fits into the function of biblically-based counseling as it does into preaching. Even if it refers to preaching, the inclusion of "exhort," clearly encompassing the element of coming alongside to aid,[18] indicates that exhortation is the kind of preaching that speaks sensitively to recovery issues from a biblical perspective.[19]

It turns out, therefore, that the classic biblical section on Scripture's inspiration is not only inspiring regarding the principles of recovery, but is also inspirational for those doing counseling/therapy related to recovery. It helps provide the needed correction and adequacy for those who later find themselves patiently seeking to help heal the deep pain of their brothers and sisters in Christ.

Beginning the Process of Piercing Application[20]

Most evangelicals would render lip service to the importance of the application of biblical and theological truth. Not nearly as many have thought through the process of the application of Scripture.[21] And far fewer have considered how difficult application can be when people become depressed or disillusioned.

The amazing way in which the writer of Hebrews applies Psalm 95 to the circumstances of his readers is a classic biblical example of piercing application. Those whom he addressed, almost certainly from Jewish backgrounds, were clearly emotionally disillusioned with Christianity and drifting spiritually (Heb. 2:1–4).[22] Persuading them to internalize and act upon the proper application would be difficult. The author chose to do this by demonstrating that Christ was superior to their old life as Jews. Psalm 95 illustrates that many in David's day (Heb. 4:7) had made the same mistake of hard-heartedness toward the Lord (Heb. 3:8, 15; 4:7; cf. Ps. 95:8). It also speaks of events that took place while Israel was in the wilderness of Sinai after the exodus (under the leadership of Moses) and reflects on the corporate choice of that generation of Jews to harden their hearts toward God and forfeit the rest that lay ahead in the Promised Land (Heb. 3:11). This implies that the outlook of the readers of Hebrews was nothing new. It had happened before when there was disillusionment under Moses and David in the Old Testament era.

Applicationally, the answer was the same in all three cases, just as it is today. Instead of hardening their hearts, the Jews needed to respond positively "today" by doing the exact opposite—opening wide the thoughts and intentions of their hearts to the Word of God (Heb. 4:12).

But this does not mean that the Word will simply apply itself! It does mean that, when the standards of the Bible are used to judge a person's innermost thoughts and emotions (Heb. 4:12) and bring the improper or distorted aspects under the spotlight (v. 13), momentum shifts in the direction of full-blown application. Choosing to display this kind of piercing honesty today is just as crucial when the recovery issues are deeply buried within. While this is not the entire applicational process, it is usually the hardest and most decisive step.

Learning from the Sins of the Fathers

Some in counseling may think that the field of psychology initially understood the devastating emotional impact of a distorted family of origin on creating recovery needs in the next generation. This is not the case. In the Bible the sinful pattern of parents is seen as early as the book of Genesis. It is not necessary to look any further than Isaac following in the steps of Abraham's lies (Gen. 12:12–19; 20:2–16; 26:7–11), followed by Jacob's pattern of deceitfulness and a host of lies by his sons in relation to selling Joseph into slavery. References are also made in the Ten Commandments to God "visiting the iniquity of the fathers on the children, on the third and fourth generations" (Exod. 20: 5; Deut. 5:9).

In other words, the sins of the fathers will be reproduced in the succeeding generations unless there is a major turnaround of obedience to the Lord (Exod. 20:6; Deut. 5:10). Unfortunately, these passages do not indicate how the cycle of family sin can be broken. They merely observe what happens if the sinful family pattern is not somehow stopped: The sin will cascade down through the generations of the family, proliferating ongoing problems, just as it did in the Old Testament.

The outlook of the New Testament toward such Old Testament examples (1 Cor. 10:6) is much more hopeful, though. While their actions were branded as evil (1 Cor. 10:6–11) and the strong tendency to fall by repeating such behavior was stressed (v. 12), there was also a promise that God, because of his faithfulness, would provide the way of escape in each instance of temptation (v. 13). "Escape" here meant the end or successful outcome[23] and likely implied more than just standing firm in a single instance of temptation. Because the passage emphasizes sinful patterns of behavior, the escape probably was from similar patterns. What tremendous hope that gives in recovery—the confidence that the Lord is providing a way out of the background patterns that have haunted lives!

Truthful Living with Unanswered Questions

While the Lord has seen fit to reveal to us everything that we need to know, he has not seen fit to tell us everything we want to know, much less everything on any subject. We are, after all, finite creatures and could not perceive much of the knowledge—whether biblical-theological or in the specialized psychological realm of recovery—if God did give us access to it.

The perspective that the Lord wants us to have on what we don't know as well as what we do, is found in Deuteronomy 29:29. Sandwiched in the middle of a discussion of the covenant that God was renewing with Israel, including an extensive listing of consequential blessings and curses (Deut. 28), this verse contrasts "the secret things" and "the things revealed." God has imparted "the things revealed" for the purpose of obedience to him and behavioral impact, not just understanding. (This dovetails beautifully with the practical purpose of Scripture detailed in 2 Timothy 3:16–17.) But mankind has no claim on "the secret things" because they "belong to the Lord our God."

For the study of theology, this means that no system will ever be exhaustively comprehensive and fill in every pigeon hole in the systematic framework. As far as recovery is concerned, we will have to learn to live with some unanswered and perhaps troubling questions, trusting the Lord to make available to his people what is sufficient for undertaking the biblical recovery process.

Where Often Is Heard an Encouraging Word

Because of the emotional pain and depression attached to recovery issues, the setting for recovery is often discouraging. From a biblical-theological recovery angle, this should not be the case. If anything, the tone of the recovery environment should be like the wording of the western song, "Home on the Range," "where seldom is heard a discouraging word." But this does not go far enough. In recovery, the phrase needs to read, where *often* is heard an *encouraging* word.

Romans 15:4–5 tells us that such encouragement, as well as the perseverance to see through a painful and trying process like recovery, is available in the Bible:

> For whatever was written in earlier times was written for our instruction, that through perseverance and the encouragement of the Scriptures we might have hope. Now may the God who

gives perseverance and encouragement grant you to be of the same mind with one another according to Christ Jesus.

This passage is a fitting way to close this chapter because of its emphasis on unity being the outcome of perseverance and encouragement. Since those two factors are very important, for Christians in general and for those in recovery in particular, they serve as common ground.

Evangelical recovery programs must look more toward biblical-theological truth while believers in the Christian community must more readily accept recovery as biblically viable. As this happens, the dynamic duo of scriptural and personal resources for encouragement and perseverance can make a positive difference in both settings.

3

The "Father Figure" of Biblical Recovery

The parent-child bond is powerful. How much more powerful it is between God and His children. We need to tap into the deep roots of our parental bond with God. We need to draw out all the emotional richness that gives vitality and passion to this utterly holy yet remarkably down-to-earth Father. . . . And we need to be motivated by the knowledge that God is a Father who will embrace us with the words, "I'm proud of you. . . ."

Phil Davis
The Father I Never Knew:
Finding the Perfect Parent in God

CAN YOU IMAGINE getting at least a shadowy look at what everyone who comes through an airport checkpoint has crammed into a hand-carried bag? Such a job would rarely cease to be interesting, if not outright comical or astounding. What does being able to giggle or grimace at the contents of these items have to do with the theology of recovery? It is a helpful comparison to God, who sees a lot more clearly than a scanner, a lot more broadly than carry-on luggage, and a lot more constantly than a checkpoint. This is the infinite kind of God evangelicals believe in and worship, who is the Author and Finisher of the process of biblical recovery as well as faith (Heb. 12:2 KJV).

Does Anyone Really Know and Care about Me?

Our society is highly impersonal. The Internal Revenue Service, the Department of Motor Vehicles, banks, schools, and stores have succeeded in virtually reducing us to numbers that generate sophisticated computer form letters. Weeks, even months, may go by when the closest thing to a personal touch is a form letter or a nonaggressive telemarketer. When our large and powerful institutions are so distant and impersonal, it is difficult to believe that God, who is infinitely bigger and more powerful, could really care about us and our individual problems and needs.

This difficulty is compounded when we have a background of recovery issues. Rebounding from trauma or shame, feeling individually significant, and trusting anyone are tall orders for such people, even in reasonably good circumstances. Doing so in the dehumanizing environment that is inexorably invading our lives is much tougher yet. Under the circumstances, it is quite natural to feel that nobody really knows us or cares about us.

However, the words of Psalm 139[1] leave little doubt that God cares for us and knows much more about each of us than we know about ourselves. The writer refers to God having searched him and known him (v. 1), as understanding his thoughts (v. 2), and as being intimately acquainted with all his ways (v. 3). The Lord knows it all (v. 4) but still does not reject us for our flaws and mistakes. In a very real sense, this means God cares about you.

It is supremely important in recovery to know that someone cares and will be there no matter what. This is exactly how the psalmist describes God: He is there, wherever we go (vv. 7–12). This remains true even when the dark parts of life are about to overwhelm us (v. 11), a figurative expression for depression.[2]

For some in recovery, it is doubly difficult to accept caring and concern in the present because of abandonment in the past. This comes into play wonderfully in Psalm 139 as well. The Lord is not only there for us now, he always has been! Verses 13–18 beautifully describe God's active and loving involvement in each mother's pregnancy and his intricate planning of each life, even before it comes about (v. 16). Among other things, those plans include adopting every Christian into his family (Gal. 4:5–6), as we will discuss later.

This is the God of a balanced evangelical theology.[3] This is also the God who can anchor the biblical recovery process as the stable, trustworthy, loving, and accepting Father those people never had at crucial stages of their development.[4] Yet, unlike the God-as-you-understand-him approach of the Twelve Step programs, the biblical God is not shaped by our likes and dislikes and does not subjectively sacrifice his true righteousness, holiness, or transcendence.

Omni-Love, Acceptance, and Reality

These caring characteristics of God seen in Psalm 139 form only a small portion of the formal theological consideration of the attributes of God.[5] While somewhat artificial, these attributes are often separated between those related to God's perfection (or moral attributes) and those related to God's infinity (or omni-attributes).

There certainly is a sense in which perfection and infinity seem like apples and oranges, but in terms of basic understanding, this breakdown is useful enough. While such theological distinctions may sharpen our intellectual understanding, it must be questioned how much they enhance our personal identification and relationship with the Lord.

To maximize the relational side of things (which is so crucial in recovery), it may be just as valid to say, in kid's terms, that each of God's attributes is as big and strong as it can be. Such a description may lose some of the element of abstract precision, but it gains a lot in terms of concrete approachability, and that is a highly significant gain for those who tend to feel distanced from God already.

Let's consider the ramifications of this trade-off. Is it a departure from orthodox theology to discuss the divine attributes in other than a basically compartmentalized abstract manner? If not, what are the dangers involved in approaching the character of God from a more personal angle?

First, it would not seem to be placing an orthodox evangelical theology of God in tension at all to simply organize and approach the biblical material and specific theological concepts from a more personal angle. Admittedly, there are dangers, but they are not insurmountable. The subtle tendencies to select only the specific attributes that appeal to someone as approachable or to overemphasize the immanence (i.e., nearness, closeness) of God and underemphasize his transcendence (i.e., infinite greatness) can be held in check, if there is a constant awareness of these dangers.

Since turnabout is fair play, it is also worth asking whether it is accomplishing all that theology should by retaining the traditional sterile approach. Is it really edifying holistically (i.e., to the whole personality), or merely satisfying intellectually, to dissect God's attributes in a way that has marked similarities to studying a cadaver in a medical classroom?

The danger of slicing up the character of God into categories and attributes is that you lose a sense of the whole. And, in the case of God's character, the whole is definitely greater than the sum of the parts. It is the whole of God's character that we must relate to, not just, say, one characteristic per day or situation. The attributes are very important qualities, but they can never be separated from the harmonious symphony that is the unified divine character. Thus, it is just as dangerous to pick apart the character of God, even for the purpose of better understanding, if it is not put back together with an emphasis on the living, personal Whole that balances the emphasis on separate characteristics.

Having said all this, it also seems perfectly legitimate to reshuffle the way that attributes have been discussed, if there is good reason to do so. For example, the concept of perfection sets off alarms with most people in recovery because perfectionism is a common part of the recovery profile. Thus, it might be preferable to shift consideration of the perfection attributes to omni- form, which would emphasize God being totally big and powerful (to strengthen the weak), rather than perfect and never-erring (underlining the imperfect and failing).

Think about it. Is it not much more personal and approachable to speak of God's omni-love (which never runs out), instead of his perfect love (which we can never attain), even though his love *is* perfect? The same thing could be said for several other attributes. Would it be improper to speak of omni-reality and omni-acceptance as attributes of God? Perhaps reality should be subsumed under truth and acceptance under grace, or something similar. Still, there is something very positive and exciting about the ideas of omni-reality and omni-acceptance, especially for those in need of recovery.

Before concluding this discussion of how the attributes of God relate to recovery, it is worth noting the wondrous balance[6] in God's character. There are numerous vantage points from which that balance is seen. For example, God's justice and mercy balance each other perfectly, as do his transcendence and immanence, as well as his sovereign choice[7] and his creation of mankind with the true responsibility and choice he has granted us.

Perhaps the most striking indication of the breathtakingly beautiful balance in God's character is seen in John 1:14. When Jesus Christ, the unique Son of the heavenly Father, came into the world to demonstrate his Father (v. 18), he was characterized as "full of grace and truth" (v. 14). No other human who has ever walked this earth can claim to be full of either grace or truth.

As far as humankind in general is concerned, this pairing of grace and truth is incredibly good news. It is not that grace and truth are never paired off in life, but it is increasingly rare. Someone has actually and graciously offered us the salvation that we could never deserve (Eph. 2:8–9), while still embodying the truth in the fullest sense of the word (John 14:6)!

For people with recovery needs, however, this pairing of grace and truth seems too good to be true. They may have heard the dictionary definitions, but they did not see them anywhere in their circumstances. Instead of grace, they lived with conditional relationships, often expressed as rejection or perfectionism. Instead of truth, they got lies and had to keep highly embarrassing, frequently shameful, family secrets.

As desperately as they need the incomparable balance of grace and truth found in the heavenly Father and his Son, the Savior, it is easier said than done to get them fully receptive to the message (John 1:12). They often have to see grace and truth reflected with consistency in the lives of Christians before they can come to the point of being able to trust even Jesus Christ.

There is another side of the magnificent balance between grace and truth that must be understood. Grace backs the Lord's offer of cleansing forgiveness, while truth enables him to be totally just and righteous. He can extend mercy without, in recovery terminology, compromising his boundaries. Thus, the balance of being "full of grace and truth" (John 1:14) allows God to be God, with no tension in his perfect character.

The Perfect Adoptive Father

We have already mentioned the fatherhood of God in regard to Jesus Christ, the Son. Let us now examine the relationship between God the Father and Christians, his adopted children (Rom. 8:15–17).[8]

Less than a generation has passed since the Holy Spirit was the most overlooked member of the Trinity.[9] The impact of the charismatic movement and the emphasis on renewal in the churches have resulted in a much stronger focus on the Spirit.

As we move toward the end of the twentieth century, the Father now occupies the role of the overlooked, if not virtually ignored, member of the Godhead. Given the proliferation of divorce, illegitimate births, abuse, and workaholic and other absentee fathers, there has been a greatly diminished sense of fatherhood in our society. The question to sum up these trends is: With fathers like that, why would anyone even want to have a heavenly Father?

This general cultural disenchantment with fatherhood becomes even more complicated in recovery. Most people in need of recovery resent, even hate, the father figure in their lives, but they also desperately want to please him, no matter how lousy or abusive he may have been. It is a terribly confusing emotional double-bind. Focusing on the resentment causes guilt because of the need to please; trying to please wells up hatred because of mistreatment.

Is this resolved when a person becomes a Christian? Is he or she automatically emotionally healed so he or she can view God the Father exactly the way Scripture portrays him?[10] Very seldom, if ever. Usually the biblical data is added at the intellectual level, but the existing sense of fatherhood is not subtracted at the emotional level. As a result, the new believer looks at God the Father through a lens colored by the previous father figure(s).

This makes it tremendously difficult for Christians with recovery issues to trust the Father and to pray as if they will be heard and answered. It also tends to result in the belief that God requires some sort of legalistic performance standard. Their professed theology tells them something very different, but their emotions have not gotten the message. The warped love/hate response to the idea of father still holds sway in the emotional realm.

How can this be changed? Perhaps the most productive related theological concept that resonates emotionally is the Father's adoption of the new believer. This concept is not an easy one at any level. It implies a "Plan B" relationship because the original parents are not available. And this is exactly what must take place in biblical-recovery adoption. Against the backdrop of the dysfunctional, if not abusive or non-existent, father, it must clearly be seen that adoption by God the Father is far better, not only because he is loving and accepting but also because he will always be there and offers a security never known before.[11]

In Galatians 4:5–7 the apostle Paul beautifully describes how "Plan B" is actually "Plan A" for God the Father. All along he had been planning to adopt us. He even redeemed us out of the horrible, sinful circumstances that were spiritually our point of origin (v. 5).

But there is much more to it. With the scriptural concept of adoption (which dovetails beautifully with biblical-theological recovery), the believer can rightfully address God with "the cry of a small child to his loving 'Daddy'" (v. 6).[12] This meets a very deep need and makes possible a new, close, and satisfying relationship with God the Father.

Besides this closeness, God also declares each of his adopted children to be his heir, with all the rights and privileges pertaining (v. 7). This promise is wonderfully gratifying for people with recovery issues. Most have never had security or, if they did, it was only financial. In Galatians 4:7, the security has to do with both relationship and resources. When God the Father undertakes an adoption, he offers himself as the perfect father and all the wealth of the universe as well. No more secure relationship is possible in this life.

Perfect Insight for Forgiving Parents

Since the new heavenly Father is without a single flaw, the shortcomings of earthly parents seem even more dramatic. This can create the occasion for being even more embittered toward parents who did not meet childhood needs. It is positive for a person to be honest and fair about his or her parents' weaknesses and strengths. But it is not any more helpful to overstate their weaknesses out of anger than it is to understate or cover them up out of codependent loyalty.

What is necessary is to see the parents as they really are, and to be able to forgive them of those realistic weaknesses and the hurtful actions they committed. Until that takes place—and it may be a complex process if the wounds involved are very deep and longstanding[13]—the devil will have a foothold in the angry, unforgiving person's life (Eph. 4:26–27).

God the Father urges us to do just that, both in stated principle and in his example. Let's sample how the Father handles such forgiveness himself and how he tells us to handle it.

The Lord's Prayer in Matthew 6 includes a well-known request for forgiveness (v. 12) from the heavenly Father (v. 9). That request is based on our prior forgiveness of others who have transgressed against us (vv. 12, 14–15). He will withhold forgiveness from us if we are unforgiving toward others (v. 15). The reason is that, no matter how justified someone may feel in his unwillingness to forgive, it is, in effect, playing God to choose not to forgive. No creature has the right to ascend to God's throne and make an exception to the rule of forgiveness, just because he or she is hurt and embittered.

This point is developed in more detail in Matthew 18:21–35. There, in answer to Peter's question about how often a person should forgive a sinning brother (v. 21), Jesus answers with "seventy times seven" (v. 22), his way of expressing the idea of complete, ongoing forgiveness, or, in the words of Jeremias, "an indefatigable capacity to forgive the brethren."[14]

The force of the story that follows (vv. 23–32) is to show how much more an unforgiving person has already been forgiven by his Lord and thus how incredibly inconsistent it is not to forgive others (v. 33). The heavenly Father has every right to deal with an unforgiving person in the most severe way (v. 34). As difficult as it may be, heartfelt forgiveness must be forthcoming. There is strict accountability to the Father in such matters (v. 35).

No matter what our parents have done or the deprivation that has taken place, we must forgive. God the Father has forgiven each believer much more, and he requires it *for our own good*. It is of no benefit to have all our energy and focus riveted on the events of a past which cannot be changed but can be healed. The decision to forgive our parents (and follow-up process if necessary) is a decisive step in a healthy direction.

The Perfect Model for Parenting

Because those with recovery issues often grew up in distorted home settings, they have bad or significantly imbalanced role models for parenting their own children. The natural tendency in such situations is either to fall into parenting along the same lines despite the destructive impact of such an approach, or to swing the pendulum to the opposite extreme. Sadly, this other extreme may be just as imbalanced and unhealthy as the "same old, same old" approach.

There are two other possibilities. The first is to emulate other good Christian parents in tandem with applying biblical principles of parenting. However, since there are fewer good parenting models all the time—mostly because there are so many more people who have come out of unhealthy homes and so have not had positive parenting models themselves—this avenue may be difficult to pursue. The other alternative is to look to God the Father, the perfect parent. The only time the Father could even be accused of not being there for his Son had to do with the cross and Jesus' words, "My God, My God, why hast Thou forsaken me?" (Matt. 27:46). But that rhetorical question was the fulfillment of the prophecy in Psalm 22:1 and in no way represents the kind of abandonment seen in recovery profiles.

Does this seem odd, to observe and emulate God as the model parent? It didn't to the biblical writers. For example, in Matthew 7:7–11 the subject of prayer (vv. 7–8) leads into a telling discussion of how parents answer their children's requests (vv. 9–10). The passage is crowned with a comparison between human parents, who can be very evil, and the heavenly Father, who will always give what is good to his children (v. 11).

The point here is not just listening to your children, answering their requests for their good, and providing for their physical needs. Other aspects of the way the Father parents must be added to get a complete picture or model. One of the most important is his repeated strong affirmation of his Son, Jesus Christ: "This is My beloved Son, in whom I am well-pleased" (Matt. 3:17; 17:5).[15]

People in recovery may not be able to become "heavenly" parents, but they can make substantial progress by emulating God the Father and observing biblical limits. By doing so hand in hand with their own recovery process, the sins of the fathers do not have to continue unchecked into their children's marriages and parenting.

The Perfect Example of Harmonious Relationships

Most Christians believe the Trinity is a cardinal doctrine of the faith that must be believed but has no practical application. This is understandable, since the "tri-unity" of God (i.e., three persons who are one God) is usually presented in a highly abstract manner. But such an outlook is far from balanced and leaves the unfortunate impression that God is abstract and impractical. This misconception is deadly to those with recovery issues who already tend to feel that parents and other authority figures don't care and won't be helpfully involved in their lives. This impractical concept of the Trinity can stifle an essential close relationship between the recovering believer and the trinitarian God.

A balanced perspective acknowledges the Trinity as the classic model of harmonious relationships.[16] The Trinity can, thus, readily be applied to the need for harmonious marital and family relationships and, although not the primary focus here, to relationships within the family of God, the church.[17]

This can be seen even more clearly when the major building blocks of the orthodox doctrine of the Trinity are presented. Evangelicals clearly agree that (1) there is one God (Deut. 6:4), reflecting the need for unity for harmonious relationships; (2) three distinct Persons are called "God" equally (Matt. 28:19), implying equality of persons in healthy relationships; and (3) though equal, each of the three Persons plays a different, but complementary, role in the Godhead (1 Peter 1:2), leaving little doubt that their unity and equality still allows for individual diversity and different roles. Since each of these three building blocks is vitally important to the overall understanding of tri-unity, departure at any point moves the resulting formulation outside (or, at least to the extreme edge) of the bounds of orthodoxy.

Table 3.1 parallels the standard categorized departure from the three major tenets of trinitarian theology seen in historical theology and what would be its corresponding practical heresy. Departure from the belief in one God usually takes the form of *Tri-theism* (belief in three gods). It overplays the reality that three are called God, while underplaying the fact that Scripture never says there is more than one God. Relationally, over-playing to the individual and underplaying to the family unit

Table 3.1
Applying the Trinity's "Boundaries" to Recovery

Doctrinal Point	*Historical Departure**	*Relational Departure*
One God	Tri-theism	"Lone Ranger" individualism
Three Persons, who are equally God	Subordinationism	"One up, one down" relationships and roles
Each Person plays a different role	Unitarianism (Arianism, Socinianism, etc.)	Egalitarianism (genders and roles)

*For the reader desiring further information, each of these departures (and their various historical expressions) are discussed in detail in standard church history and historical theology texts, as well as theological dictionaries.

creates an isolated individualism, which, from a recovery perspective, is often not only very lonely, but also terrified of emotional intimacy.[18]

Subordinationism is the departure from the belief in the equality of the three Persons called God. Here, one or more of the Persons is superior and/or inferior. The difference in roles each Person occupies is wrongly assumed to indicate higher and lower rank among the three. This relational parallel is an unhealthy dictator-doormat approach to the family, whether it be the husband seeing himself as higher than the wife or the parents making the children feel inferior. Even in typically hier-archical subcultures, such superior/inferior attitudes can cause tremendous emotional damage.

Failing to hold to the foundational truth that each person plays a distinct role usually results in a kind of *Unitarianism,* that only one God exists, though he may go by three different names. This comes about by allowing the truth of monotheism (one true God) to swallow up the equal importance of the distinct personhood

of the Father, Son, and Holy Spirit. Relationally, radical egalitar-
ian feminism lurches far to the side of the undifferentiated equality of the genders (Gal. 3:28) and does not recognize the foun-
dationally created distinctions between men and women. It is an
imbalanced overreaction against the extreme hierarchicalism
mentioned above and often results in either tremendous anger
or confusion about healthy biblical gender roles.

Learning to Trust the Father's Plan

It can be great comfort for a believer to realize that, as the
old spiritual says, "(God's) got the whole world in his hands."
This can be even more true for people with terribly painful
backgrounds, who tend to feel like the world around them is
completely out of control.

Scripture promises that "God causes all things to work
together for good to those who love God" (Rom. 8:28). But we
must be careful before using this passage to comfort a hurting
believer. Counselors and ministers must be biblically astute
and emotionally sensitive enough to realize that this passage
emerges in the context of suffering, confusion, and weakness
(vv. 18–27). Also, they must be honest enough not to leave the
impression that everything working together for good means
everything always works out in a pleasant manner for Christians. This is not dealing in reality, either in life or in Scripture.
The good that all things are working toward (v. 28) is confor-
mity to the image of Jesus Christ (v. 29). All the wording
included in verses 29–30 points toward Christlikeness.

So, no matter what a person has been through, he or she can
take heart that the Lord's promise is still in effect. The Father figure of recovery is not asleep on the job. He is using everything,
including the shameful and painful occurrences in our lives, to
smooth away the rough edges and to mold each one into greater
and greater resemblance to Christ. There are no wasted, throw-
away people or events!

4

The Biblical Basis
of Recovery

[We believe] in one Lord Jesus Christ, the only-begotten
Son of God, begotten from the Father before all time, Light
from Light, true God from true God, begotten not created,
of the same essence as the Father, through Whom all things
came into being, Who for us men and because of our salvation came down from heaven, and was incarnate by the
Holy Spirit and the Virgin Mary and became human. He
was crucified for us under Pontius Pilate, and suffered and
was buried, and rose on the third day, according to the
Scriptures, and ascended to heaven, and sits on the right
hand of the Father, and will come again with glory to judge
the living and the dead. His Kingdom shall have no end.

A portion of the Nicene Creed, A.D. 381

The Person of Christ

The orthodox church, from the Apostolic Age through the
present day, has made the unique confession that God himself entered the human race and provided the way of salvation.

63

The Second Person of the blessed Trinity wrapped himself in humanity and redeemed sinful human beings by paying a debt they could not pay. The purchase price was nothing less than his own blood, which he willingly shed upon the cross.

When the apostle Peter wrote to encourage the persecuted Christians in Asia Minor, he told them that they "were not redeemed with perishable things like silver or gold . . . but with precious blood, as of a lamb unblemished and spotless, the blood of Christ" (1 Peter 1:18–19). Peter went on to remind these harassed, first-century saints that through Christ they had become believers in God. Therefore, their faith and hope were to rest in him (1 Peter 1:21).

Like those faithful believers before them, the early church fathers, who were also persecuted in their own day, set their faith and hope in God and stood firm in his truth concerning his Son. Their faith was expressed in the Nicene Creed, a testimony to the world that God exists and that he had done an extraordinary thing on mankind's behalf.

The New Testament writers and the early church fathers together point us to Jesus Christ and urge us to believe in him. They consistently present to us the unique God-man who is the Savior of the world, the Lord of the universe, and the One who alone is worthy to be worshipped.

But the apostles and the saints of old do not offer to us a divine Savior who is out of touch with the human beings he came to redeem. On the contrary, they teach us about the God who fully entered into the human experience: He was born; he experienced joy and suffering; he died and rose again victoriously, conquering death and securing eternal life for all who would believe in him.

Jesus Christ, the perfect and sinless Son of God, identified with us in our humanness. This remarkable truth revealed to us in the Gospels should greatly comfort those of us who wrestle with recovery issues. Jesus knew the countless difficulties people face in their daily lives. He saw with his own eyes the various life situations causing suffering, desperation, and heartache. He even knew from personal experience how troublesome the family could be at times.

Having been raised in a godly, but imperfect family, Christ understood the problems that can arise out of this close relationship. While he was never physically or emotionally abused by his family, he was often misunderstood and ridiculed by them, for they did not, in the beginning, understand his identity or his mission (Luke 2:49–50; John 7:5).

Opposition and ridicule were nothing new to Jesus. He had to endure much of these from the Jewish religious leaders during his earthly ministry. But what probably grieved him the most was the scorn he encountered from his loved ones. On one occasion, while he was ministering to a large crowd, his family went to take charge of him because they thought he was crazy (Mark 3:20–21). In another incident, his brothers' unbelief manifested itself when they urged him to go and perform his miracles for the world (John 7:1–5). They thought he was aspiring to become a renowned public figure.

Many of us may have also been habitually misunderstood and ridiculed by our family members. We may have been accused of being insane because we were exercising our unique abilities in a way that didn't fit their mold. We can be encouraged by knowing that Jesus understands from his own experience our hurt feelings stemming from painful criticisms. Furthermore, he is at work in us to enable us to endure and overcome these relational conflicts.

There is a great lesson for us to learn from the family aspect of Jesus' earthly life. Despite the intense opposition, Jesus continued to live in accordance with God's will. Eventually, his family came to believe in him (Acts 1:14). Because he held steadfast to his heavenly Father's will, his loved ones finally recognized his true identity and mission. His obedience ultimately opened their eyes to the truth. Jesus is our example and model, teaching us and empowering us to remain true to God's will even in the face of unjust treatment.

Unlike Jesus' family, however, our loved ones may never come to believe in us or our Savior. Nevertheless, because we are committed to him, sooner or later they will have to realize how our lives have changed for the good. They eventually will see, to some extent, that steadfast obedience to the Son of God brings wholeness and recovery. Our identity and mission are wrapped up in him. The risen Christ makes himself known through the transformed lives of his people. He will become visible to our loved ones through the continual healing of our wounds. This is an essential part of the Lord's ongoing ministry in the church.

The Mission of Christ

In Luke 4:18–19, Jesus explains the nature of his God-ordained ministry by quoting from Isaiah 61. The people, gathered at the synagogue in his hometown of Nazareth, were mesmerized as they heard him describe his mission:

> The Spirit of the LORD is upon Me, because He anointed Me to preach the gospel to the poor. He has sent Me to proclaim release to the captives, and recovery of sight to the blind, to set free those who are downtrodden, to proclaim the favorable year of the LORD.

Indeed, this was a message of good news and recovery to a people who were weary, distressed, and weighed down with all kinds of burdens. For three years or more Jesus ministered to these disheartened people, fulfilling his divine mission. He taught about the kingdom of God (Mark 1:15); he cast out demons (Mark 1:25–26); he healed the sick (Mark 1:32–34); he made blind eyes see, deaf ears hear, dumb tongues speak, and paralyzed legs walk (Mark 2:11; 7:32–35; 8:22–26); he raised the dead and he forgave sins (Mark 2:8–10; 5:35–43).

He came "to seek and to save that which was lost" (Luke 19:10). He came forth from the Father to recover the human race, which had gone astray. He entered into this sinful world to become our compassionate Shepherd and to lead us to God's healing pastures. In every respect, his was a message and ministry of recovery.

Jesus Christ identifies with us in our pain and suffering. The Book of Hebrews says he entered into our suffering that we might be made one with him. "For both He who sanctifies and

those who are sanctified are all from one Father; for which reason He is not ashamed to call them brethren" (Heb. 2:11). His
mission of mercy and his identification with our distress united
us into one spiritual family.

His earthly ministry is proof not only of Jesus' divinity and
messiahship but also confirmation that God cares about his
people and desires to make them whole. Christ's ministry did
not stop when he ascended into heaven. It broadened.

The Lord Jesus is at work in his church today, touching
people by his Spirit and through the spiritual gifts he has
bestowed upon his people.[1] His mission is also continuing in
the three roles he established during his earthly mission:
Prophet, Priest, and King. Let us examine how these three functions of Christ offer further insight into his perpetual ministry
and give special hope to recovering believers.

Prophetic Ministry

As Prophet, Christ continues to reveal the Father to us. While
on earth, he made the truth of God known through his teaching, character, and actions. On the night before his crucifixion, he prayed for all future believers saying that he would continue to make the Father known to them so that God's love
may dwell in them and that he himself may be in them (John
17:20–26).

Through his prophetic ministry, Christ also reveals to us the
special relationship we have with himself and his Father. God
has not left us alone to face the hardships of life (John 14:18).
He is intimately connected to us because we believe in his Son.

In addition, Jesus carries on his revelatory work through the
Holy Spirit, our Helper and Comforter (John 15:26). Christ
communicates God's love to us through the Holy Spirit and
impresses into our hearts the reality of this divine communion
(Rom. 5:5; Eph. 3:14–21).

To sum up, the recovering believer is known by God. God
will not abandon that which is his own. Christ continues to
impress the reality of this special, intimate relationship
between God and the believer. This is important because many

believers suffering with recovery issues can trace some of their problems back to abandonment (e.g., an absentee father).

High Priestly Ministry

The Book of Hebrews discloses Christ's role as High Priest. The writer points out the weaknesses and temporal nature of the Levitical priesthood in order to elucidate the superiority and permanence of Christ's priestly ministry. The author describes in detail Christ's holy character and the ongoing service he performs on behalf of those who believe in him.

First, this heavenly Priest "had to be made like His brethren in all things, that He might become a merciful and faithful high priest in things pertaining to God, to make propitiation for the sins of the people" (Heb. 2:17). He was made like us in every way. He was severely tested during his time on earth. He experienced temptation in his suffering, yet was without sin. And he suffered even to death. Therefore, even though he now dwells in heaven, Christ is able to help us in our trials and temptations (Heb. 2:18) and to sympathize with our weaknesses (Heb. 4:15). He also invites us to his throne of grace to find strength in our time of need (Heb. 4:16). Through these aspects of Christ's priesthood, we are given permission to be open and honest with him. As we reveal ourselves to him, we will find a merciful, faithful, and sympathetic Advocate who can identify with us. We can approach him truthfully, with freedom and confidence.

Second, Jesus is alive forever, "hence, also, He is able to save forever those who draw near to God through Him, since He always lives to make intercession for them" (Heb. 7:25). Christ, our heavenly Intercessor, is on our side. Aware of our weaknesses and sin, he stands in the gap for us, speaking to the Father on our behalf.

The apostle Paul also describes Christ's role as our Intercessor, but explains Jesus' intercessory work from a different perspective, showing how the Father willingly gave his Son to make the divine/human relationship possible:

What then shall we say to these things? If God is for us, who is against us? He who did not spare His own Son, but delivered Him up for us all, how will He not also with Him freely give us all things? Who will bring a charge against God's elect? God is the one who justifies; who is the one who condemns? Christ Jesus is He who died, yes, rather who was raised, who is at the right hand of God, who also intercedes for us.

Romans 8:31–34

This is a powerful and comforting truth for those who have experienced rejection and abandonment. God is with us, and he will never leave or forsake us (Heb. 13:5–6). We must humbly and reverently accept Christ's intercessory work on our behalf, recognizing our utter inability to plead our own case. Admitting our powerlessness to make ourselves acceptable before God is the first step toward truthful living.

Lastly, "while we were still helpless, at the right time Christ died for the ungodly" (Rom. 5:6). Our divine High Priest offered himself as the supreme sacrifice, making perfect forever those of us who are being made holy (Heb. 10:14). Unlike the Levitical priests, Jesus offered one sacrifice, and his work was finished (Heb. 10:11–12). Christ accomplished his work and sat down at the right hand of the Father (vv. 12–13). He is our faithful High Priest who sacrificed his own body to make us holy, who intercedes for us, and who sympathizes with our weaknesses.

For those of us who were raised in homes where we had to perform in order to gain acceptance and approval, this is a very difficult truth to grasp. But our minds can be transformed by God's Word (Rom. 12:2). We come before God, not on our own merit, but on the basis of Christ's work. His blood paved the way for our acceptance, and he stands before the Father on our behalf. The Lord does not weigh our deeds on heavenly scales in order to see if we measure up to his standard. His holy requirements were met in Jesus Christ.

We must now, by faith, rest in God's presence (Heb. 4:1–11). We can approach God unashamedly and fully assured, knowing that Christ made us acceptable. God loves us for who we are because we have accepted his truth.

Kingly Ministry

Before Jesus was conceived, the angel, Gabriel, announced to Mary that her firstborn son would be a King. He was to be given David's throne, and he would reign over the nation of Israel forever (Luke 1:32–33). Christ also knew that he was born to be a King and confessed this truth to Pontius Pilate (John 18:37). At the crucifixion Pilate had this written charge nailed above his head: "JESUS OF NAZARETH, THE KING OF THE JEWS" (John 19:19).

But Christ's kingdom and rule extend far beyond the borders of Israel. He is Lord of the universe with all powers and authorities, in heaven, on earth, and under the earth in submission to him (Eph. 1:19–23). He is not only head of the church, but every person who has ever lived will eventually answer to him, including Pilate and the religious leaders who had him crucified (Phil. 2:9–11).

The ultimate heavenly Authority was judged and condemned by the supreme earthly authorities of his day. This is an amazing irony. But Jesus willingly submitted himself to those worldly powers in order to further identify with the ones he came to redeem. Christ well knows what it is like to be abused and mistreated by authorities. Therefore, we know he can empathize with those of us who have been treated with contempt by the authority figures in our lives and we can rest assured that our benevolent Ruler will always deal with us justly and fairly.

In summary, Christ understands our human flaws and weaknesses and possesses the power to change us. He works in our lives through the Holy Spirit and through his roles as Prophet, Priest, and King. He continually reveals the Father to us so that we might know his love; he intercedes for us as our faithful and sympathetic High Priest; and, as our benevolent King, he rules over us with kindness and understanding. Our response to these glorious truths about Christ should be growth in child-like trust and steadfast obedience.

The Redemptive Work of Christ

Apart from the incarnation, the atonement of Christ is prob-ably the most mysterious and unfathomable concept in the study of theology. How could one man's shed blood cleanse the entire human race of its sin? Why did Christ have to suf-fer such awful torment in order to reconcile mankind to God? Why did God not simply forgive the human beings he created?

Theologians have been asking these questions for centuries. Some have vigorously studied the atonement and scoffed at its absurdity. Others have fallen on their knees in reverence and awe, thanking God for his salvation. There really is no middle ground. Either one believes and accepts it as God's truth or rejects it because the concept seems irrational and unbelievable.

The atonement of Christ should not be taken lightly. Not only is a person's eternal destiny determined by what he or she believes about Jesus and his atoning work, but his or her emo-tional and spiritual health is also at stake. Those of us who have accepted God's truth concerning the death and resurrection of his Son have an eternal home with him and have begun the spiritual and emotional journey toward recovery.

The Lord Jesus humbled himself and became a servant to mankind in order to bring people back to the God who cre-ated them. When we consider the person, ministry, and aton-ing work of Christ, we begin to understand the severity of our spiritual condition. Isaiah, who spoke of Christ seven hundred years before his birth, portrays Christ and his mission in these words:

For He grew up before Him like a tender shoot, and like a root out of parched ground; He has no stately form or majesty that we should look upon Him, nor appearance that we should be attracted to Him. He was despised and forsaken of men, a man of sorrows, and acquainted with grief; and like one from whom

men hide their face, He was despised, and we did not esteem
Him. Surely our griefs He Himself bore, and our sorrows He carried; yet we ourselves esteemed Him stricken, smitten of God,
and afflicted. But He was pierced through for our transgressions,
He was crushed for our iniquities; the chastening for our well-
being fell upon Him, and by His scourging we are healed. All of
us like sheep have gone astray, each of us has turned to his own
way; but the LORD has caused the iniquity of us all to fall on
Him.

Isaiah 53:2–6

In his account of the passion, Matthew demonstrates the
fulfillment of Isaiah's prophecy by vividly describing the events
surrounding Christ's crucifixion. First, Jesus agonizes in prayer
alone in the garden of Gethsemane because his disciples could
not tarry with him (Matt. 26:36–46); he is betrayed by Judas,
one of the twelve (Matt. 26:47–56); he is brought before the
Sanhedrin, unjustly condemned and beaten (Matt. 26:57–68).
Then Peter, one of Jesus' closest disciples, publicly denies him
three times (Matt. 26:69–75). Christ is brought to trial before
Pilate who tries to release him but is forced to condemn him
due to the intense opposition of the people (Matt. 27:11–27).
Finally, he is handed over to the Roman soldiers who mock
him, spit on him, and beat him (Matt. 27:27–31).

All of these events take place in less than twenty-four hours.
But the persecution does not stop here. He is to experience the
entire weight of human wickedness and the full force of God's
wrath against sin upon the cross. All the powers of hell are
unleashed upon the sinless Son of God as he hangs there upon
that wooden cross. Our finite minds can never fully comprehend the suffering he endured in those anguishing hours.

The people who passed by the crucifixion site, probably some
of the very ones he had healed, mocked Jesus and jeered at him
(Matt. 27:39–40). The religious leaders and teachers of the Law
taunted and degraded him (Matt. 27:41–43). The criminals who
were crucified with him also hurled insults at him (Matt. 27:44).

Then came the final and most heartrending blow. Darkness
descended upon the entire land as God the Father poured out

his wrath. The blackness could be felt, and it caused the Son of God to gaze up into the heavens and cry out, "My God, My God, why hast Thou forsaken Me?" (Matt. 27:46). Shortly after this statement, having experienced physical, emotional, and spiritual torment to the fullest, he breathed his last and died (Matt. 27:50).

Jesus Christ identified with us in our sin and faced its ultimate consequence—death. In his death he entered fully into the darkest side of human experience. He understands, in the most intimate way, what it is like to be victimized. He knows the pain of a broken heart. He was betrayed, deserted, falsely accused, beaten, mocked, spit upon, abandoned, and forsaken by God. He experienced an aloneness in his death we will never be able to comprehend.

Thankfully, the story does not end with his tragic death. B. B. Warfield reminds us that "our Lord did not come into the world to be broken by the power of sin and death, but to break it. He came as a conqueror with the gladness of the imminent victory in his heart; for the joy set before him he was able to endure the cross, despising shame (Heb. xii.2)."[2] He won a decisive victory for us in his death and resurrection. Through faith in him, we can overcome (1 John 5:3–5).

All of the divine purpose and every aspect of the human experience converge at Christ's cross. At the cross, God's character is fully revealed: his holiness, righteousness, justice, sovereignty, faithfulness, mercy, love, and compassion. The sinfulness and value of the human race are also evident. Physical, spiritual, and emotional suffering are clearly displayed. Humiliation, abandonment, pain, and abuse in all their ugliness are unveiled at the cross before the watching world. Lastly, divine forgiveness, empathy, and compassion are manifested and offered to every human being who would come and kneel before him at his cross. The divine/human relationship begins afresh at Christ's crucifixion, and the road to recovery will lead us there over and over again.

On the other hand, the resurrection of Christ brings to light victory, joy, peace, acceptance, and reconciliation with God and with each other. The resurrection gives us eternal hope. It is the promise of complete healing and recovery. All of life is wrapped up in the person and work of Jesus Christ. He provided the way of salvation in order to lift us out of our meaningless existence.

The death and resurrection of Christ are much more than a historical fact. They are a living reality because he is a living reality. Christ fully identified with us in our human condition. When we consider his cross and empty tomb, we must see ourselves there with him (Rom. 6:1–14). We must realize who we are. It is the only pathway to truthful living!

5

The Indwelling Counselor in Recovery

Romans 8:26 assures us that "Likewise the Spirit also helps in our weaknesses. For we do not know what we should pray for as we ought, but the Spirit Himself makes intercession with groanings which cannot be uttered." The founders [of Alcoholics Anonymous] used the phrases a power greater than ourselves and God as we understood him. That phrasing stops short of meeting core spiritual needs since He is not "as we understood him" but as He has revealed Himself. . . . Without spiritual growth, there is no recovery.

Robert Hemfelt, Frank Minirth, and Paul Meier
Love Is a Choice: Recovery for Codependent Relationships

SILENCE CAN be golden. When something very important needs to be articulated, though, silence is fool's gold. It is a vacuum that needs to be filled in the right way, because it will inevitably be filled by whoever or whatever opportunistically recognizes the inviting emptiness.

Unfortunately, the position of much of the evangelical Recovery Movement on the role of the Holy Spirit in recovery could aptly be termed loud silence. The above quote from *Love Is a Choice*[1] is one of the very few statements that can be located in print about the Holy Spirit from principal evangelical recovery writers.[2]

This situation is highly ironic when the trend across the board in evangelical circles in the past generation has been exactly the opposite. The Holy Spirit, who not long ago languished in the virtual obscurity of being the so-called overlooked member of the Trinity, has been brought into the spotlight at center stage by the charismatic and renewal movements. Thus, the near silence about the Spirit in the evangelical Recovery Movement is decidedly against the grain of wider evangelicalism but may be largely explained by the honest, haunting question asked recently by Archibald Hart: "How does the work of God through his Holy Spirit relate to the work we do in counseling?"[3]

The reason for the deafening silence may be based on either ignoring the importance of the Spirit (though that importance is well known) or mistakenly thinking the Spirit has little, if anything, to do with recovery. We would certainly hope that the reason is ignorance or mistake. If, however, it is consciously ignoring the key role the Spirit plays in all spiritual growth, then it is a working perspective that is very near to naturalism and very far from evangelical essentials. If the problem is related to ignorance or mistaken surface integration, then the viewpoint and omission in counseling/therapy can be corrected largely through learning and applying to recovery a correct biblical pneumatology (i.e., doctrine of the Holy Spirit).[4] Still, for whatever reason(s), if the Spirit is absent from the recovery treatment process, a huge price is being paid: For all practical purposes, "there is no recovery."[5]

This chapter will seek to make available to all evangelicals—whether counselors, those in recovery themselves, or Christians who simply wish to understand the interface—how the various contours of the doctrine of the Holy Spirit relate to recovery.[6]

When All Is Chaotic, the Spirit Is There

From the beginning it has been "the Spirit who holds things together."[7] At that early stage there was not yet sin or even the finished creation. But the Holy Spirit was already moving in the darkness (Gen. 1:2) to prepare for the light to break in (v. 3) that the good (v. 4) might begin. That role of the Spirit has continued, in a manner of speaking,[8] but with even more of a personal touch. Now, as the impact of sin is felt painfully throughout the created order until its final recovery[9] (Rom. 8:18–22), the Spirit goes beyond keeping things together by letting things fall apart.

The good news is that the Spirit is still there to help at the deepest emotional level (vv. 23–27). It is not necessarily bad news that suffering and weakness get the best of a situation. Such a sense of weakness (v. 26) is a good indication that a person has, at least to an extent, hit bottom. This means that the person may have come to that difficult, but decisive, point at which he or she is finally willing to look beyond personal resources to find help (i.e., recovery).

This passage offers help in prayer when someone is so overwhelmed he or she does not even know how to pray about things (vv. 26–27). The Spirit accurately portrays to the Lord what is in the hurting believer's heart and is invariably able to bring those requests in line with God's will (v. 27). In other words, the Spirit can pray more effectively for the needs and hurts in a believer's life than the person can, since there are so many cases where a Christian does not know how to pray according to the Lord's will. Believers with recovery issues should be very thankful that the Holy Spirit is always available to pray when they are overwhelmed by the pain in their lives.

However, as table 5.1 makes clear, there is much more about the Spirit's wider ministry to rejoice over. This listing of the ministries of the Holy Spirit indicates that the Spirit is at work from before the point of conversion until the Christian is finally (and eternally) in the Lord's presence. The ramifications of these ministries for biblical-theological recovery will be the focus of each remaining section of the chapter.

Table 5.1

The Work of the Holy Spirit and Recovery

Spirit's Ministry	Time Frame	Parallels in Recovery
Convicting	Before/after conversion	Denial
Indwelling	Point of conversion	Intimacy/acceptance
Adopting	Point of conversion	Abandonment/identity
Baptizing	Point of conversion*	Belonging
Sealing	Point of conversion	Security
Gifting	Point of conversion**	Significance/self-image
Counseling	Throughout Christian life	Healing/accountability
Praying	Painful times/suffering in Christian life	Being overwhelmed or unable to function
Filling/Fruit	Throughout Christian life	Empowering/healing relationships
Transforming	Until earthly life ends	Completion of recovery

*It is, of course, realized that many charismatic evangelicals, citing passages like Acts 1:5 and 2:4, believe that the baptism of the Holy Spirit is closely related, if not equated, to speaking in tongues and is a subsequent, repeated experience after conversion. The position presented in this chapter represents the mainstream orthodox position in church history and the majority evangelical position today.

**Some evangelicals take passages like 1 Timothy 4:14 to indicate that spiritual gifts can be bestowed after conversion by the "laying on of hands" by Christian leaders. The majority evangelical position, however, is that laying on hands is the point of recognition of calling and giftedness by the Lord.

The Spirit and Soft-Heartedness toward God

Before explaining the conviction of the Spirit, let us consider why such conviction is necessary. One central Old Testament passage and a related New Testament passage will be briefly examined.

The Old Testament section is Ezekiel's version of the New Covenant prophecy found in Ezekiel 36:23–27.[10] After describing how the house of Israel profaned God's name (v. 23) and was guilty of filthiness and idolatry (v. 25), the prophet gets to the heart of the matter: the sinful nation's "heart of stone"

(v. 26) that must be replaced with a "new heart" and a "new spirit" (v. 26).

The agent God deploys to soften up his stone-hearted people and to empower them for obedience to his standards is the Holy Spirit (v. 27). The people of Israel may have been tough nuts to crack from a human standpoint, but their hard hearts would be like butter melted by a microwave oven when the Lord applied the promises in this prophecy.[11]

In the New Testament this same problem is seen in the vivid incident where Stephen becomes a martyr because he tells the truth about the religious leaders "always resisting the Holy Spirit" (Acts 7:51). He also describes their strong, consistent resistance as being spiritually "stiff-necked and uncircumcised in heart and ears" (v. 51).

The Holy Spirit had been promised in relation to the New Covenant in order to soften hearts toward God (Ezek. 36:26–27). The New Covenant had been ratified in the redemptive work of Christ (Luke 22:20). But the hard-heartedness continued with a vengeance (Acts 7:51–60).

What does all of this mean? It is called denial in recovery circles. In counseling, denial is a tenacious unwillingness to admit that something is gravely wrong with you or your family and take responsibility to move in the direction of resolution (i.e., recovery). People in denial have hardened their hearts toward God, as well as to their inner pain or relational dysfunction. That is why the Holy Spirit has been made available as the New Covenant era heart-softener. Further, even after the vise grip of denial has been broken, the power of the Spirit is needed as much or more to reorient lives to healthy patterns of obedience to the Lord (Ezek. 36:27). The latter part of this chapter will deal with that part of the Spirit's work in the recovering believer's life.

Conviction: Spirit of Truth, Spirit of Persuasion

Elsewhere in the New Testament (John 16:8–13) the Spirit's job as heart-softener is referred to as conviction in a judicial sense.[12] The term employed in John 16:8 (Gk. *elenchō*) elsewhere (for example, Ephesians 5:11) also means "bring to light," "expose," "set forth," and "point something out to someone."[13] The various nuances are appropriate not only for initial conversion but also for recovery.

At first glance it seems that John 16:8–11 is only related to the conviction of unbelievers so they might become Christians. That is, of course, an absolutely crucial function for the Spirit to accomplish since non-Christians have the built-in resistance factors of spiritual blindness (2 Cor. 4:4) and deadness (Eph. 2:1). But there would seem to be a much wider application to the conviction of sin, righteousness, and judgment than just entering new life in Christ, the starting point of full-blown biblical recovery.[14]

Certainly sinners must come to the point of owning up to their sin (including unbelief in Christ) in comparison to the absolute righteousness of the Lord Jesus and the judgment that inevitably waits if the unbelief continues (John 16:9–11). However, it is little less important at many other junctures to admit sinful unrighteousness in the face of the Lord's standards and the long-term consequences of continuing the habitual, sinful behavior.

Admittedly, this may be more of an application of John 16:8–11 than its direct interpretive intent, but its practical legitimacy is strengthened by what follows in verses 12–13. The same "Spirit of truth" (John 14:17; 15:26; 16:13) that convicts the unbelieving world to come to a proper understanding of their doomed spiritual status outside of Christ also must stretch the understanding of those who are already believers (vv. 12–13).

Generally, "what is to come" (v. 13) has to do with future disclosures of a prophetic nature.[15] However, the description of not being able to "bear" (Gk. *bastazō;* "to endure"[16]) something that needs to be said (v. 12) and the revealing of "all the truth" at a later point (v. 13) parallels what usually takes place in recovery. After denial is finally shattered, people with recovery patterns must progressively face as much of the truth about their backgrounds and sin as possible, though they usually are not able to bear all the pain at once. But it must come out if emotional healing and healthy relationships are to materialize to a substantial degree.

Parakletos: Infinitely Big Shoes to Fill

The same section of the Gospel of John introduces and repeatedly refers to the Holy Spirit as the *paraklete* (John 14:16, 26; 15:26; 16:7). The term means "counselor," though it may also mean "legal advisor" much like the modern sense of counselor/therapist.[17]

The counseling role of the Spirit would be difficult, but it was made more so by the fact that he was coming to take over the "practice" formerly occupied by Jesus Christ. The Spirit was called another Counselor (John 14:16) because Christ had already been functioning as the prophesied "Wonderful Counselor" (Isa. 9:6).

Though both are equally God, one major difference between the counseling ministries of Christ and the Holy Spirit stands out. Christ could be seen and related to in essentially the same way as any other human being. He talked in an audible human voice. The Holy Spirit cannot be seen and normally does not speak audibly.

Nevertheless, the Spirit is a very effective Counselor. If anything, as we will see in the next section, the Spirit develops an even closer relationship with the counselee than Christ did. He is also available to help people cope and grow over the long term ("forever"; John 14:16) while Christ had to ascend to the Father (vv. 2–3). It may be frustrating not to see and hear him, but the good news is no one needs an appointment or has to worry about being cancelled because of a scheduling conflict.

Indwelling: My Heart, the Spirit's Home Office

A former pastor and Fuller Seminary professor, Robert Boyd Munger, authored an influential little booklet titled "My Heart, Christ's Home." This same idea can be applied to the Holy Spirit, only the Spirit's indwelling is more like a home office than a residence.

The first passage in John's Gospel predicting the indwelling of the Spirit indicates that the Lord intended his presence to provide a sense of intimate acceptance by the Lord (John 14:17–18). Not only would he be as close as close could be (i.e., indwelling the believer's life; v. 17), but he would be there to counter any possible thought that Christ was abandoning his people in ascending to the Father (v. 18). Quite the contrary! Jesus was leaving his beloved ones in infinitely capable hands.

This indwelling of the Holy Spirit also carries with it a built-in sense of accountability. For example, 1 Corinthians 6:18–19 argues against immoral behavior by a Christian because "your body is a temple of the Holy Spirit who is in you" (v. 19). The Spirit's presence came through the priceless redemption of Christ (v. 20). Proper appreciation should be shown to the Lord by glorifying him in what is done with your physical body (v. 20).

The point here is that the Holy Spirit is with the Christian wherever he or she goes. This presence is much more than the Secret Service guarding a United States president or the undercover police tailing a prime suspect. Any thoughts or actions contrary to a lifestyle glorifying the Lord are immediately known. This is not legalism—it's accountability that can keep the recovering believer on the road of true spiritual growth.

Adoption: Feeling Like a Rightful Heir

Some of the best parents we know have adopted their children. Similarly, some of the most appreciative children we know have been adopted. Unfortunately, it is not automatic that such parents or children will appreciate, or live out, their roles as they should. They may have no realistic sense of what to expect.

However, things can be much better in a believer's adoption by the Lord (Rom. 8:15–16; Gal. 4:5–7). For one thing, the "spirit of adoption" (Rom. 8:15) knows exactly what he is doing. There is absolutely no reason to think the Holy Spirit will fumble his part in the spiritual adoption process. The Spirit's adoption proceedings are linked to simultaneous rulings (in the highest court in the universe) in which each newly adopted child of God is named a full-fledged heir (Rom. 8:16–17; Gal. 4:6–7). The Lord is willing to give adequate evidence to his child that he or she is greatly loved and fully accepted, a fact believers with recovery issues have found in very short supply in their lives.

Spirit Baptism: That Deeper Sense of Belonging

When the baptism of the Spirit became a historical reality on the day of Pentecost (Acts 1:5; 2:4), there was no way to know exactly what to expect. John the Baptist had predicted its coming but had only contrasted it with his own water baptism (Matt. 3:11).[18] Jesus had told his apostles before his ascension to stay put until the Spirit baptism came (Acts 1:5). About all that can be gleaned is that Pentecost began the corporate worship and fellowship of the New Covenant church (v. 42) in earnest. Those who received the message preached by the apostle Peter were all baptized in short order (v. 41) and were immediately characterized as being together and of one mind (vv. 44, 46). Thus from day one, the baptism of the Spirit was related to togetherness and belonging in Christ's church.

The only undisputed teaching passage on the baptism of the Holy Spirit is 1 Corinthians 12:13.[19] This key verse draws implications from Acts 1–2 and applies them clearly to the setting of the body, one of the apostle Paul's favorite analogies for the church.[20]

Sandwiched between affirmations of the unified diversity of the body of Christ (1 Cor. 12:12, 14), verse 13 deals with two important dimensions: ethnic background ("whether Jews or Greeks") and economic status ("whether slaves or free"). As Davis aptly observes, "All Christians, despite the inequities of their former existence, have now been brought into one body . . . by a common experience of the Spirit in baptism."[21]

In the body of Christ every person is on level ground spiritually. This is very comforting to know, especially for those with recovery issues who are probably not on a level playing field with healthy believers in terms of immediate growth potential. Thus, because other factors of diversity may also come into play, it is absolutely imperative for recovering Christians to know in the deepest part of their hearts that they belong because they are Spirit-baptized (1 Cor. 12:13).

Sealing: Security in the Spirit

Our candidate for the most underrated ministry of the Holy Spirit is sealing. Many treat the Scriptures on the sealing of the Spirit as if it were the sealing of an ordinary plain white envelope instead of a person's life for time and eternity. They think that the sealing of the Spirit is no big deal. Such an attitude, however, is a serious mistake theologically and even a worse error from a biblical recovery angle. For those who come from a background in which family members have demonstrated a pattern of making promises but never following through, the sealing of the Spirit is God's guarantee that he will do exactly what he has promised.

Three passages in Paul's letters tell of the Holy Spirit's ministry of sealing. Both 2 Corinthians 1:22 and Ephesians 1:14 speak of the Spirit's sealing as a "pledge" (Gk. *arrabōn*), meaning "first installment," "deposit," or "down payment."[22] Ephesians 4:30 adds the behavioral ramifications of this sealing which continue until the believer is in the Lord's presence on the final day of redemption.

When someone gets involved in a rental or leasing contract, he is normally required to put down a deposit to demonstrate good faith that the payments and stipulations in the agreement will be carried out. In essence, the Lord has contracted with each new believer at the point of faith in the gospel message (Eph. 1:13). The duration of the contract is until "the day of redemption" (Eph. 4:30), meaning the down payment of the Spirit's seal remains in force until then.

There isn't much security in life now with an unpredictable economy, tremendous international political instability, freeway driving, and the like. Yet in spite of this pervasive external insecurity, as well as the gnawing internal insecurity of recovery-related issues, lifelong security is the possession of the believer who carries the Holy Spirit's seal of approval.

Charisma: Spiritually You're Gifted and Significant!

Many school systems now offer honors classes and programs for those whose test scores rank them as gifted and talented.

This small percentage of young men and women are supposedly the best and brightest of our student populace. These classes are designed to challenge them to even greater achievements in their training and stronger contributions to our society in the time ahead.

Theoretically, such programs seem valid. After all, to place students who are bored because things are too easy with those who are struggling to survive does seem ludicrous. Such considerations may not, however, tell the whole story. Many exceptionally bright students simply do not fare as well because of test anxiety, learning disorders, being late bloomers, and a host of other valid reasons. Further, such programs can be footholds for arrogant elitism in our schools. Finally, extensive research and experience have shown that, in most cases, it is the good student, not the exceptionally bright one, who over time becomes the best adjusted and more productive worker.

Not only should these factors cause our society to rethink its approach to educating gifted students, they should give the evangelical church pause in the way it deals with spiritual giftedness. Presently, many local churches and other ministries tend to recognize people as gifted because they manifest certain spotlighted gifts or because they are particularly skilled in using those spectacular or appreciated gifts.[23] Is such an outlook either biblical or healthy?

The limited number of doctrinal passages on spiritual gifts in the New Testament cuts across the grain of any spiritual elitist mentality that might develop (Rom. 12; 1 Cor. 12–14; Eph. 4; 1 Peter 4). Since no two passages list the gifts in exactly the same order (or even exactly the same gifts for that matter), it is presumptuous to view some gifts as more important than others.[24] Admittedly, some spiritual gifts are under the microscope in certain passages, but this is because of their localized abuse (1 Cor. 13–14) or necessary leadership in the healthy growth of the body (Eph. 4:11–16). A balanced perspective on spiritual gifts—especially needed to get believers with recovery profiles headed in the right direction—must recognize three often-overlooked points: (1) their gracious origin; (2) their individualized manifestations; and (3) their twin big-picture purposes.

First, because of the normal translation as "spiritual gift," one would expect that the Greek word used would be *pneumatikos,* as in 1 Corinthians 12:1. However, the standard Greek term in the spiritual gifts passages is *charisma,* literally rendered "a gift freely and graciously given," in this case "special gifts . . . bestowed by the grace of God."[25] Thus, it is not valid for Christians to take credit for their giftedness or the impact of the use of the gift(s) because it is due to the Lord's undeserved grace.

Secondly, the virtually unnoticed truth in 1 Corinthians 12:4–6 is that God's allotment of spiritual gifts is tied to the kinds of service in which the gifts are employed and even the impact or effects of the gifts' usage. This means that there is absolutely no legitimate basis for comparing Christians and their spiritual gifts. Such comparison is not only egotistical, it is also an implied criticism of the divine Gift-giver, who graciously allots and links gifts, ministries, and their outworking.

Finally, one of the tandem purposes of spiritual gifts is seen in the following phrase: "the common good" (1 Cor. 12:7). Though these gifts of grace do endue the believer as a gifted, significant member of the body of Christ (vv. 12–27), they are not intended by the Lord to be used for personal gratification but rather for corporate unity and edification (vv. 25–27). The other overarching purpose of the gifts is to glorify God in their use (1 Peter 4:11).

All in all, the gifts of the Spirit found in 1 Corinthians 12:7–11 have suffered almost as much abuse at the hands of imbalanced evangelicals as have believers with recovery issues. Evangelicalism can become considerably more balanced by viewing spiritual gifts as the Lord imparting to each of his children unique giftedness and significance. Recovering Christians can best fit into the church and grow in the context of such a thoroughly biblical perspective.

Filling: Energized with Wisdom and Power for Recovery

Over the last generation the filling ministry of the Holy Spirit has received as much attention as sealing has received little. However, one key biblical case study of the filling of the Spirit has still not received adequate attention: Stephen, the early martyr (Acts 6–7).

In the limited space given to Stephen's ministry and death, his effectiveness is attributed three times to the filling of the Spirit (Acts 6:5, 10; 7:55). He is also expressly said to be full of "faith," "grace and power," and "wisdom" (vv. 5, 8, 10).

This close association between being full of the Spirit and full of faith, power, and wisdom has tremendous ramifications for recovery. People with recovery backgrounds almost always have great trouble with trusting, feeling empowered, and feeling intelligent and capable enough to make wise decisions. So the filling of the Spirit can be a wonderful ally in the recovery process. Not only are trust, empowerment, and wisdom skills to be learned through recovery therapy, they are also the outworking of dependence upon and control by the Spirit, much like Stephen experienced.

Filling Meets Fruit: Energized for Recovering Relationships

Ephesians 5:18 is the didactic passage on the filling of the Spirit that balances the narratives in Acts. This verse contains the direct command to "be filled with the Spirit," given in vivid contrast to the negative illustration of drunkenness. But this verse weaves together with the ensuing section all the way down to Ephesians 6:9, and this is a fact that is frequently overlooked. This is a huge oversight because Ephesians 5:19–6:9 illustrates how the filling of the Spirit works out in fruitful primary relationships (with God and other Christians; wife-husband; child-parent; employee-employer) on a day-to-day basis (Eph. 5:19–33; 6:1–9).

The primary section on the fruit (a harmonious unity[26] of attributes) is Galatians 5:22–23.[27] But many do not look far enough here either to discover what happens to the fruit over the long term. Scripture tells us that if there is a fruitful life (vv. 22–25), there will be a wonderful harvest at the end (Gal. 6:8–9).

These two contexts offer great hope for recovery. It is possible to repair damaged relationships in the power of the Holy

Spirit (Eph. 5:18–6:9). The kind of love, patience, and self-control needed to rebuild healthy and joyful relationships can be harnessed through the fruitful filling of the Spirit.

The Spirit of Glorious Transformation

The harvest of a life of walking in the Spirit will not only be fruitful, it will be absolutely glorious! All who are children of God, regardless of their backgrounds, are on the glory road (Rom. 8:16–18, 21, 30) in the power of the Holy Spirit.

This is where we're headed. In the meantime, however, there is the matter of the general suffering of the Christian life and the specific pain of full spiritual recovery. Those who have already suffered a great deal of pain can take heart in the fact that all believers will, along the way, eventually come to understand that pain, because suffering is a realistic aspect of Christian living (vv. 17–18).

Progress in the Christian life and in biblical-theological recovery is much more than suffering, however. It is also a supernatural liberty available through the Spirit (2 Cor. 3:17). And it is a progressive transformation into the image of the Lord due to the energizing of the Holy Spirit (v. 18). If we had spiritual X-ray vision, we could watch ourselves grow up into the Lord's glorious image. Fortunately, along the way we can be encouraged (2 Cor. 4:16) because the affliction we must work through now is lightweight in comparison to the heavyweight eternal glory awaiting us at the end of the transformation process.

6

Biblical Self-Image

Man, in contrast from all the rest of creation, has not merely been created by and through God, but in and for God. He is, what he is originally, by God and through God; he is also in and for God. Hence he can and should understand himself in God alone. Just as it is said of no other creatures, "let us make," so also it is said of no other that it has been created "after his likeness" or "in his image."

Emil Brunner
Man in Revolt

Human Beings as God's Unique Creation

The creation account recorded in the first chapter of Genesis reveals that God created mankind on the sixth day after he had called into existence the heavens and the earth, filled with every living thing. The human being was the last living creature God created before his Sabbath rest.

When considering the place of human beings in the sequence of creation, we might think we were an afterthought. After all, if we were picked on the sixth day of team tryouts for softball or volleyball, wouldn't it seem as if we really didn't matter, as if we weren't really that valuable? Many of us have been in this situation. We were simply chosen because no one else was left, and the quota had to be filled. In this world, to be picked last can leave us feeling unimportant, unwanted, and worthless.

However, in the creation account, God had a different reason for creating human beings last. They were not an afterthought. They were not beings he created just to fill up the empty space on earth. On the contrary, their last-place position reveals their significance, dignity, and purpose.

Human beings are the apex of God's creation and the crowning glory of his handiwork. After breathing the breath of life into the man and woman, God commissioned them to rule over his creation. Then "God saw all that He had made, and behold, it was *very* good" (Gen. 1:31, italics ours). Human beings were to be his representatives on earth, governing his creation under his sovereignty. With the making of the man and woman, God's work was now complete.

Since the early nineteenth century, when Darwin's theory of evolution was accepted as the scientific explanation of humankind's existence, the reality of who we are and why we exist largely has been lost. Evolution devalues life. It robs us of our worth and dignity as God's unique creation because it takes away our true purpose for living, which is to be in and for God. Unfortunately, Christians are not immune to the influences of this intellectual ideology.

Many of us were raised in homes that did not acknowledge God and by parents who did not value us as human beings. Like the evolution theorists, our parents taught us by their actions that we were an accident, were worthless, and had no purpose. Therefore, we struggle with self-esteem.

The term "self-esteem" carries with it a negative connotation for many in the church today. This is not without good reason. Some believers have abused the concept and by doing so, have justified their self-centered living. However, having a healthy view of oneself and being a believer in Christ are not incongruent, as long as we understand the basis of our self-worth.

As Emil Brunner so aptly stated, "[Man] is, what he is originally, by God and through God; he is also in and for God. Hence he can and should understand himself in God alone."[1] We owe our existence to God. We must understand our worth in relation to him.

Biblical self-worth is rooted and grounded in God. Unbiblical self-worth is founded upon the values of this fallen world. The self-worth the world often propagates is based on the lies of evolution, which say that one must create his or her own worth. Human beings have no inherent value, so they must create their own.

Ultimately, this teaching drives people to despair because they soon realize their utter inability to create their own value and worth. There are too many forces working against them, from within and without, and no genuine power within themselves to produce real change. Only God, who is the foundation of self-worth, can create and build a healthy personality. But often, to the people's own detriment, they thrust his truth behind their backs.

Unfortunately, many Christian self-help groups and recovery programs do not emphasize this vital connection to God. As a result, believers are left in the dark about who they really are, and they become frustrated with their lack of growth.

We must begin our recovery process with God and apply what his Word reveals about us as his special creation because only then will we find true healing. We are God's unique creation because we are the only beings created in his image and likeness. While his image in us is now marred by sin, it is still in place, and it still constitutes the essence of our being.[2] We were not an accident nor were we an afterthought designed to fill the empty places of the earth. Each individual is known by God and has incredible worth to him.[3]

Because of the immense importance of these divine truths, we need to examine the image of God in us and explore our unique relationship to him. Through this, we will begin to understand our relationship with others, ourselves, and creation and how these relationships affect our self-image.

A study like this poses a special problem for those who have been raised in a sin-ladened, dysfunctional home. Those childhood experiences and the way they have affected our present lives can thwart our acceptance of God's revelation. Because the emotional part of our hearts often speaks louder than the rational side of our minds, the lies we grew up with seem more of a reality to us than God's truth.

Nevertheless, God is able to break through the past deception clouding our judgment and the mist shrouding his path to healing and wholeness. He does this by giving us new experiences that cause us to grow in his likeness. Through prayer, his Word, and his Body, he helps us to grow and enables us to respond to our past in a healthy way that glorifies him. Thus, we are gradually transformed, and we begin to reflect more clearly his image in us.

Therefore, in order to engage in truthful living, we must integrate God's truth about ourselves into our daily lives. We must possess his reality and make it our own. Then we will begin to shed the lies from the past and live authentically in Christ in the present. This chapter will offer some practical ways to apply God's truth. For now, let us turn to the specifics of his revelation concerning human beings.

Human Beings in God's Image

There has been much debate and discussion throughout the centuries concerning what it means to be created in the image and likeness of God. This present discussion will not solve this complex mystery, but it will lay a foundation and enable us to further understand our true origins. Just as it is important for us to discover the effect our families of origin have had on us in terms of recovery issues, so it is just as crucial for us to understand how God has shaped us by stamping his image in us at creation.

We can begin by discussing what the image of God in human beings does not mean. It does not mean that we are omnipotent, omniscient, sovereign, or infinite.[4] These are qualities theologically referred to as God's nontransferable attributes. No one can possess these characteristics but God alone.

Righteousness, holiness, rationality, will, self-awareness, personality, creativity, spirit, the ability to think, feel, and relate were qualities given to us by God. They represent his image in us. This image is not something we *have*, as if it was an addition to human nature. It is who we *are*. The image of God is the essence of our being. By our existence, we are in the image of God.[5] These qualities, inherent in human nature, set us apart from the rest of creation.

While we have possessed these characteristics from the beginning, we did not experience them to their fullest capacity, even before the fall.[6] God intended for us to grow and mature into these attributes that represent his likeness in us.[7] While we are still capable of growing and maturing in some of these areas[8] even after the fall, sin has perverted this growth process. The ability and desire to grow is a God-given aspect of human nature; it is not a result of the fall. But sin entices us to grow in the wrong direction.

How does growth and the image of God relate to recovery and truthful living? The sin-induced conflict within us coupled with a nonempathic family of origin environment can lead us down a path of destructive living, further away from the true aspects of God's image in us. Thus, we grow in a way that is contrary to God's will. Because of sin, rebellion against God's will is a universal problem; however, those who have lived in an abusive situation are likely to experience more intensely this willful growth against God's will.

In other words, growth is normal. It is a fundamental aspect of being human because we are not omnipotent and omniscient like God. But deviant growth (growth that is contrary to God's will) often results in recovery-related behaviors (e.g., obsessive/compulsive, codependency, and boundary problems) and is not in line with God's revelation of the human being, even though this kind of existence may seem normal to those who have experienced habitual abuse. Recovery issues rob us of our true humanity by causing us to surrender our God-given characteristics associated with his image in us. These aberrant behaviors conceal God's image in us.

God created all of us with personality, rationality, will, and the ability to think, feel, and relate. We are unique people capable of God-centered growth and maturity, but we must first regain our true identity as people in his image.

Human Beings in Relation to God

Jurgen Moltmann insisted that we understand human beings in their relationship to God rather than in their relationship to the rest of creation. He also pointed out that "likeness to God is a theological term before it becomes an anthropological one. It first of all says something about the God who creates his image [us] for himself, and who enters into a particular relationship with that image, before it says anything about the human being who is created in this form."[9]

God created human beings in order to relate with them. We know this because, down through the centuries, he has revealed himself to various people (such as Cain, Noah, Abraham, and Moses); he has revealed himself in his Word and through his Son. He has made himself available to us (Acts 17:27). If he did not do this, we would have had no way of knowing the one true God—or our true selves.

God also uniquely created human beings with the ability to hear him, love him, and obey him. Ultimately, this is the whole purpose of our existence. By his grace, even the fallen human soul is capable of this divine communion. In our relationship to God, we begin to see who we really are. We were not made to live apart from him.

Many of us have never learned how to relate to other humans, much less someone we can't see! Some of us have been so abused and mistreated by people we trusted that it's hard to believe God would treat us any differently.

How do we begin to relate to God? We must begin by telling him the truth about how we feel. King David exhorts us to "trust in Him at all times, O people; pour out your heart before Him; God is a refuge . . ." (Ps. 62:8). Trust is the most difficult aspect of relating to God, especially when some of us have only known betrayal in our human relationships. But it is the risk we must take in order to find healing.

David discovered this truth over and over again. In Psalm 31, when David had been forsaken by his loved ones and was being pursued by his enemies, he felt like he was in a besieged city, cut off even from God. Yet he told God the truth, "As for me, I said in my alarm, 'I am cut off from before Thine eyes'; Nevertheless Thou didst hear the voice of my supplications when I cried to Thee" (v. 22).

"If the LORD had not been my help, my soul would soon have dwelt in the abode of silence. If I should say, 'My foot has slipped,' Thy lovingkindness, O LORD, will hold me up. When my anxious thoughts multiply within me, Thy consolations delight my soul" (Ps. 94:17–19). These are the words of a man grieved by the evil surrounding him. But, because of his honesty with God, he found what he needed in the Lord's unfailing comfort.

The rich blessing of God's presence in the midst of abandonment awaits those who are willing to cry to him and trust in him. Through honest prayer, we can begin to build a relationship with our Creator to restore in us a sense of who we truly are and what we were intended to be before the fall. Reconciliation to God through Christ begins to reverse the effects of the fall and opens our hearts to the true meaning of our existence. In him alone do we find life and wholeness.

Human Beings in Relation to One Another

As the image of God in us is manifested more clearly through our relationship to God, so do we reflect his image in our relationships with one another. As God is a relational being, so we were created to relate with him and with one another.

We learn about ourselves as we relate with one another. In our human relationships we discover that we are valuable, but we also realize that we can be deeply hurt. These pleasant and painful interactions are necessary for our maturing process.

How we handle them will determine if our growth is God-centered or not.

There is no escaping the fact we need each other. Human beings cannot survive in isolation. We need the validation of our existence that comes from mutual fellowship. Hendrikus Berkhof has pointed out that "God is not a solitary being, and a man created in his image is not at home in solitude. Man as an isolated unit can not express the image of God."[10]

The image of God is only fully represented in the community of believers. Consequently, when we were called into fellowship with God, we were also called into fellowship with one another. The New Testament bears out this truth in a multitude of "one another" passages. For example:

"be devoted to one another" (Rom. 12:10)
"give preference to one another" (Rom. 12:10)
"be of the same mind toward one another" (Rom. 12:16)
"love one another" (Rom. 13:8)
"accept one another" (Rom. 15:7)
"but through love serve one another" (Gal. 5:13)
"be kind to one another" (Eph. 4:32)
"confess your sins to one another" (James 5:16)
"pray for one another" (James 5:16)
"love one another from the heart" (1 Peter 1:22)

If the church were to follow the biblical mandate revealed in these "one another" passages, it would be much healthier and there would be less of a need for professional therapists and counselors.[11]

Paul said in the Book of Romans that "we, who are many, are one body in Christ, and individually members of one another" (Rom. 12:5). God is able to work through the members of his body to bring healing to those who have need. Even in our own pain God can use us to minister to someone else and, in the process, restore us. That is the beauty of relating to one another as brothers and sisters in Christ.

However, many of us have been hurt or abused by members of the body. Maybe our parents brutally mistreated us in the name of Christ. After such devastating ordeals, it is very hard to trust again. It takes a long time to heal from these deep wounds. But the truth is that not everyone is like our former abusers. We must risk again in order to achieve the truthful living we desire.

We can begin by taking our situation to the Lord in prayer and asking him to guide us to a church or a group of people with whom we can build healthy relationships. God is faithful and he will lead us to safe pasture. But we must do our part to be obedient to the "one another" passages and reach out to others. It will be difficult and time-consuming, but God will strengthen the willing heart.

Human Beings in Relation to the Self[12]

Since the fall, human beings have become somewhat of an enigma—not to God but to ourselves. Separation from God has left our personalities fragmented and split. We often do not understand ourselves. The Bible does not speak directly to our relationship with ourselves, but it is obvious from the way it describes us that there is good reason for the personal confusion residing deep in our souls.

First, we are of infinite value to God (John 3:16; Matt. 12:12; Luke 12:24), but we are also insignificant (Job 4:19; Isa. 40:22). We are to have dominion over the earth (Gen. 1:26; 9:2), but we are weak and frail (Ps. 49:12; 103:14). We are preeminent (Ps. 8), yet sinful (Gen. 6:5; Isa. 53:3). We are mortal (Ps. 49:10; Heb. 9:27) yet immortal (Rom. 2:7; 2 Tim. 2:10). We are both physical (Gen. 2:7) and spiritual (Prov. 20:27; James 2:26).

Fallen human beings are a paradox. It's no wonder we are often a mystery to ourselves! The biblical description of man reveals why we must have a vital connection to God. We need him to put us back together again and define who we really are. Otherwise, we are hopelessly lost in the sea of self-doubt, searching endlessly for an identity we are not equipped to find on our own.

When we come to God, he begins to integrate our fragmented personality. He reveals our sin and weakness and changes our priorities for living. This is a painful, lifelong process that will not be complete until we are taken up to glory. However, this does not mean that we will not experience any significant change in this earthly realm. The benefits in this present life far outweigh the pain affiliated with this sanctifying process.

We know we are moving toward God-centered maturity when we encounter the suffering associated with the healing of our sin-stained personality. The apostle Paul describes the suffering he and his companions endured while ministering in the province of Asia. He says that it was far beyond their ability to endure, so that they despaired even of life (2 Cor. 1:8). Nevertheless, this happened that they might not "trust in [themselves], but in God who raises the dead" (v. 9). God was shaping their personalities through their suffering, causing them to mature in Christ. In the same way, God can use our present afflictions to integrate us and bring us to maturity in Christ.

But some of us are so filled with self-hatred and self-contempt that we don't believe we can ever become whole. We long to feel good about ourselves, but secretly we really want to destroy ourselves. So we spend most of our time and energy running from God. The sin lodged deep in our souls keeps us from the very thing we need: wholeness, which comes from God-centered truthful living.

We will discuss more about sin, self-hatred, and the human personality in the following chapter. Self-hatred is a tormenting experience for those who struggle with it, but it is a curable predicament. The healing begins by acknowledging the problem and confessing its reality. Then we must come before the throne of grace so we can be set free to be what God created us to be, with all our unique talents and abilities.[13]

Human Beings in Relation to Creation

The fourth chapter of Genesis offers insight into what it means to take dominion over the earth. While it is clear from Cain's treachery against his brother, Abel, that sin had corrupted mankind's character, man's creative abilities were still functional. Cain built a city (Gen. 4:17). Others raised livestock (v. 20); some played musical instruments (v. 21); and still others made tools out of bronze and iron (v. 22). God intended for human beings to grow in their talents and abilities in order to exercise rulership over his creation. His image-bearers were to explore the vast riches of the natural realm and, in learning about the creation, to discover the wisdom and power of the Creator.

So human beings have grown in their abilities bestowed upon them by almighty God. But throughout history, we have used our finite knowledge for wickedness and evil, corrupting the planet by selfish endeavors. The Tower of Babel incident, where mankind desired to take dominion of heaven as well as earth, clearly demonstrates the audacity of this self-centered pride and arrogance (Gen. 11).

In many ways the human race has also become enslaved to creation, worshipping what it was meant to rule. The widespread idolatry recorded in the pages of the Bible illustrates this point. Not only was this custom an abomination to the Lord because he is the only true God, it was also a reversal of the creation mandate for human beings. God's image-bearers were never meant to bow down to images carved out of the natural order.

We might not worship overt idols in twentieth century American culture, but we often devote ourselves to the works of our hands. In our modern day this is called "workaholism." We become enslaved to our work because we idolize our performance in it. While this is a socially acceptable practice, it is yet another expression of unhealthy growth, a moving away from God's will for us. Workaholism in its various manifestations (whether job, home, or school) is a sign that recovery-related problems are beginning to surface. We might feel that we must be perfect or we will not be accepted. We could believe that performance is the basis of self-worth. Or we fear rejection, so we run from relationships and hide in our work.

Whatever the reason, the bottom line is that we are running from some deep unresolved pain. How does this relate to our creation mandate to rule the earth? When we are enslaved to this kind of existence, we are not free to grow in the abilities with which God has uniquely gifted us. Our particular job may have begun as a joyful place where we freely expressed our talents, but now, because of surfacing issues, we are driven to do it.

Workaholism—a survival technique—is a good indication that creation is actually ruling over us because we are not freely exercising our abilities to rule over it. Creativity is stifled by the need to control and conquer the environment. This includes our need to control and dominate other people, which is not a part of the creation mandate, and it is a visible sign of fear and insecurity. This is not taking dominion; rather, it is a form of slavery. We are not finding the joy of the Lord in our daily work; rather, we *must* work in order to hide from God, ourselves, and others.

We can be loosed from the bondage of workaholism by asking God to reveal to us the source of our pain. With his Spirit and the help of other people in the body, he will enable us to work through whatever the pain is. We must also become grounded in his Word, which reveals the truth of who we are as his unique creation. Through reconciliation with God, we can grow toward healthy, God-centered relationships with others, ourselves, and creation.

7

The Harsh Reality behind Dysfunctional Living

Man in reaching out for the Infinite and Absolute also starts destroying himself. When he makes a pact with the devil, who promises him glory, he has to go to hell—to the hell within himself.[1]

Karen Horney
Neurosis and Human Growth

Sin and Dysfunction

Although she did not in her lifetime profess to be a believer in Christ, Karen Horney made a profound observation concerning the condition of fallen human beings. Because of the lure of the serpent (Gen. 3), we, through Adam and Eve, chose to reach out for the glory we believed would bring us equality with God. Instead of reaching our lofty goal, however, we fell into sin. God's image in us was marred, and our relationship with him, with others, and with ourselves was severely dam-

101

aged. The alienation resulting from this experience produced a hell within ourselves.

The exercise of the human will brought us to this forsaken place of alienation.[2] The basic anxiety produced by this separation drives us to engage in certain sinful behaviors and attitudes that reflect the rebellion and conflict in our souls. Sin has pervaded every aspect of human nature. It is the true source and power behind dysfunctional living.

One cannot read a Christian self-help/recovery book and not come away with a firm understanding that we are all dysfunctional people who have been victimized by dysfunctional families. But today we are forced to ask the same question as Karl Menninger, who inquired twenty years ago, *Whatever Became of Sin?*[3]

Those in recovery circles frequently argue that the mention of personal sin only heaps more guilt upon an already guilt-ridden people. Because people have been told all of their lives how bad they are, discussing sin will only drive them deeper into feelings of depression and condemnation. For this reason, many recovery proponents determine it is preferable not to deal with sin on a personal level.

Besides, they continue, people already understand the concept of sin and its effects. To an extent this is true. Most people do understand at least one aspect of sin: that of being sinned against. The sin committed against them and its effect on them are consistent themes in recovery materials. They are also major topics in recovery groups and counseling.

Yet, because sin is represented in this lopsided manner, an implicit double standard begins to emerge among people in recovery. When hurt or abused by others, they have been "sinned against." Yet when acting out in improper behaviors or giving in to negative attitudes that hurt people, these people are not sinning, they are "dysfunctional." This imbalanced treatment of sin promotes a spiritual blindness to one's own evil.

When recovery literature masks personal sin as simply dysfunction, it does a great deal of harm. It can lead further down the road of deception and farther away from God's truth. Dysfunction, just like any physical sickness, is a result of the fall; it is not necessarily sin in and of itself. Therefore, dysfunction and sin are not synonymous terms; they have two entirely different meanings.

Dysfunction is an impairment of a specific function of the body or mind. Unlike sin, it does not carry the idea of a defiant willful act against God. For this reason, it can never be a replacement word for sin. However, this does not mean that dysfunctional is never a valid assessment of some behaviors and attitudes.

For instance, if a person is depressed because of a great loss in his life or is tormented with certain phobias, he is not "in sin" because he suffers in this way. If a person has difficulty trusting other people because she has experienced continual abuse in the past, she is not necessarily rebelling against the will of God. The Bible does not describe these emotional disturbances as transgressions against God's Law.[4] But sin, particularly being sinned against, still lies beneath the development of these emotional dysfunctions.

Sin, on the other hand, is conscious or unconscious rebellion against God and his standards. Many of the behaviors and attitudes we call dysfunction are in reality sin. Certain addictions, obsessive/compulsive behaviors, and codependencies fall into the realm of blatant sin against God.[5] The term "dysfunction" often disguises the truth of these defiant, sinful behavioral patterns. This can be a subtle and deadly deception.

The point is this: We must not confuse or blur the distinction between dysfunction and sin. Blatant sin should not be labeled dysfunction; nor should true dysfunction be considered sin. All sin is dysfunctional, but not all dysfunction is sin. Nevertheless, sin (whether it is personal sin or being sinned against) is always behind dysfunction; it is the power source that fuels dysfunctional living. Therefore, the sin factor cannot be ignored.

William Hulme, a former Lutheran pastor, discovered in his counseling ministry that an "inadequate interpretation of sin leads to an inadequate interpretation of human problems, and, in turn, to an inadequate therapy for the healing of the division within. . . . This means that any attempt on the part of the counselor to minimize sin, even with those whose sensitivity to their guilt is most acute, will slow up if not block the therapeutic process."[6]

His insightful observation certainly applies to the present-day Recovery Movement. Our intention is not to minimize the pain and anger associated with being sinned against. On the contrary, our own experience has caused us to be sympathetic and sensitive toward others who are in the midst of such suffering. We are convinced that the injuries sustained by these sins committed against us must be dealt with before we can truly come to grips with our sinful response to such abuse.

Fig. 7.1

Before the Fall

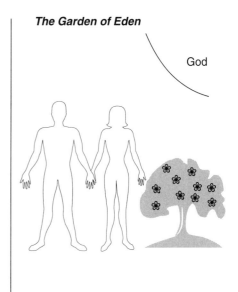

The Human Personality

Image of God

Basic motivation and attitude of the heart:
God-centered

The Garden of Eden

God

Harmonious relationship between God and human beings:
Peaceful environment

To ignore our personal sin deliberately in the recovery process will significantly hinder the healing of our divided personalities. Sin has permeated every aspect of the human personality. It has disrupted our relationship with God, others, and ourselves. Therefore, the biblical view of sin must be brought to bear on the recovery process. The power source behind dysfunctional living needs to be unveiled and shown for what it really is.

Sin and the Human Personality

Before the fall (Gen. 3), Adam and Eve lived in a garden that not only was conducive to healthy plant growth but also was a place where human beings could flourish and grow. Because of the harmonious relationship existing between man and his Creator, Eden presented an atmosphere of love, peace, and security (see figure 7.1). However, the couple's first opportunity to grow turned out to be their downfall (and ours) when they yielded to the temptation of the serpent and disobeyed the Lord's command (Gen. 2:17). As a result, they lost their moral innocence and introduced corruption and death into the human race.

What happened to Adam and Eve in this act of disobedience? Their personalities underwent a great transformation in the day of their disobedience. Being enticed to pursue what they could never attain (to be like God, Gen. 3:5), they became what they were never intended to be—shameful and guilt-ridden people who suppressed the truth by the wickedness of their pride.[7]

We can look around us and see the results of their rebellion. Pain, suffering, and death are as evident in the natural order as they are within the human experience. Wickedness and evil ripple through human history like the waves of the sea. As their distant descendants, we have inherited their sin and the inner conflict resulting from it.

In the following sections, we will explore the effects of sin on the human personality and how it relates to recovery issues. In order to develop a biblical view of sin, we will describe the process of sin in two categories: *the first non-empathic environment*[8] and *the second non-empathic environment.*[9]

The First Non-Empathic Environment

As mentioned earlier, before the fall the Garden of Eden was a place of tranquility, peace, and love, where human beings could grow in their unique abilities as they took dominion over the earth and subdued it. They could mature in godly character as they related with their Creator and with one another.

But something happened deep within their personalities when they chose to rebel against God's command. When Adam

Fig. 7.2

After the Fall:
The First Non-Empathic Environment
(God/Personal Sin)

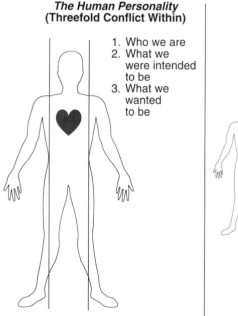

The Human Personality
(Threefold Conflict Within)

1. Who we are
2. What we were intended to be
3. What we wanted to be

The Garden of Eden

God

Basic motivation and attitude of the heart:
Self-centered

Broken relationships between God and human beings:
Hostile environment

and Eve succumbed to the temptation of the serpent and ate the forbidden fruit, their first experience was not fear of judgment. They did not run and hide out of fear that God would annihilate them. On the contrary, when they ate the fruit of the tree of the knowledge of good and evil, "the eyes of both of them were opened, and they knew that they were naked" (Gen. 3:7). Their first experience was a realization that something was wrong with them. The peace that once filled their souls was now replaced by shame.

The Lord's presence in the garden further intensified Adam and Eve's shameful experience by adding the dimension of fear and guilt. Adam's response to the Lord's calling reveals these factors, "I heard the sound of Thee in the garden, and I was afraid because I was naked; so I hid myself" (Gen. 3:10). His motivation for hiding was the wrongness that now resided in his personality. Guilt and shame had taken dominion over him.

The disobedience of Adam and Eve alienated them from God (see figure 7.2). Their relationship with him was no longer the same. Their peaceful home in the garden became for them a hostile non-empathic environment, a fearful, uninviting place that was no longer conducive for healthy, God-centered growth.

It is also apparent that their willful acts against God's command produced a threefold split within their personalities. Now existing within them was a conflict between who they were (a shameful and guilt-ridden people), what they were intended to be (a people growing in godly character as they exercised dominion over the earth), and what they wanted to be (equal to God in wisdom, knowledge, and power).

Rather than "owning" their sin and facing the guilt and shame associated with it, they chose to blame God and the serpent for what had happened (Gen. 3:12–13). This suppression of the truth about themselves and the blaming of outside forces (although the serpent was certainly guilty of wrongdoing) were the beginning manifestations of their fallen nature. The sinful nature further revealed itself in the pride, arrogance, and wickedness of their immediate offspring and distant descendants.[10]

In the first chapter of Romans, the apostle Paul eloquently exposes the sinfulness of the human heart. In suppressing the truth of God and themselves, human beings pursue their own godhood. Rather than acknowledging the one true God, which would mean facing the shame and guilt inherited from Adam and Eve, human beings have embraced the lie and proclaimed their own godhood.

The threefold conflict within the human personality, resulting from Adam's disobedience, produces in finite human beings the desire to pursue what they want to be—equal with God. Ironically, this "search for glory"[11] and godlike pursuit manifests itself in every kind of evil and perversion (Rom. 1:28–32).

As distant relatives of Adam and Eve, we have a hereditary tie to this sinful condition. The threefold inner conflict originating with them now drives us to pursue our own godhood. We, too, want to be a god. Pride and arrogance also keep us from facing the one true God and from confronting our innate shame and guilt.

Only in Christ do we begin to shed this idealized image of ourselves and become what we were meant to be: a people growing in godly character, exercising our unique abilities. When we come to Christ, God's wrath is taken away, as is the true shame and guilt associated with personal sin. Christ moves us toward what we were *meant to be* and away from what we *wanted to be*. In him, we recognize that only God can be God.

However, this does not mean that as believers we never struggle with the sinful godlike nature. Some of the old behavioral patterns will take time to break, but they eventually will be broken through the sanctification process.[12]

In summary, it must be understood that the first non-empathic environment is experienced by every human being born into this life (except Jesus Christ) because all have sinned.[13] In this sense, we are all on level ground. All humans know the inner struggle of a conscience that tells them something is wrong, even if they do not recognize this internal struggle as being a result of sin. All human beings are born alienated and estranged from their Creator. We are hostile toward God and afraid of him. Apart from Christ, the atmosphere between God and mankind is as uninviting as it was for Adam and Eve after the fall.

The Second Non-Empathic Environment

The second non-empathic environment is the category of being sinned against (see figure 7.3). Here, people are *not* on

Fig. 7.3

**The Second Non-Empathic Environment
(Human Relationships/Being Sinned Against)**

Scenes from an abusive/dysfunctional family of origin.

level ground. Because this is a fallen world, everyone knows what it is like to be sinned against; but not all people experience such sin to the same level or degree. Those of us raised in non-empathic, hostile home environments not only have to deal with the innate shame and conflict inherited from Adam, we also have an extra layer of shame, anger, bitterness, and pain stemming from various kinds of abuse. We suffer from many unmet, legitimate needs.

The Bible does not discuss the sin committed against us and its influence as much as it describes personal sin and how it affects others. But it does frequently address the need to forgive and to get rid of the bitterness, rage, and anger.[14] While unforgiveness and resentful attitudes fall into the realm of personal sin, the Scriptures seem to indicate that these behaviors are natural reactions to being sinned against.

When we come to Christ, we are reconciled to God. The atmosphere between us and him is no longer non-empathic and uninviting. Fear of judgment is replaced by security and peace. Our hostility toward God and others has been swallowed up by Christ's death. He also heals our inner conflict, releasing us from innate shame and guilt.

Nevertheless, the sinful nature we inherited from Adam and Eve remains a part of us. The sinful behavioral patterns we've learned over the years are entrenched in our personalities, and it may take a lifetime for the Lord to root them all out. Therefore, even though we are no longer under the control of sin (Rom. 6), we will continue to struggle with it until we are taken up to glory.

Many who are engaged in recovery-related behaviors do not realize the sinfulness of such conduct as codependency, obsessive/compulsive behaviors, and perfectionism. Nor do they understand that these behaviors are often fueled by a deeper well of sin, such as unforgiveness or resentfulness. Because repentance and obedience to God seem virtually forgotten concepts in Christian recovery circles, we are not exhorted to ask God to reveal to us our wicked ways. But sooner or later, we finally realize that repentance and obedience do indeed set us free from bondage and pain.

Recovery books and programs correctly inform us that we act in dysfunctional (sinful) behaviors because we are running from the pain associated with being sinned against. They often encourage us to face the pain, realize we were victimized, and get connected to safe people who will not hurt us.

We wholeheartedly agree that this process must take place. In fact, we believe that a person must first deal with the hurt and the pain associated with being sinned against before he or she can begin to explore his response to such treatment. But a person cannot do this in isolation. He or she needs the support of loving, understanding people to help get through the painful process.

We are also convinced that people will not get far in their recovery if they remain at this level of the second non-empathic environment. They will not get to the root of the problem, which lies in the realm of the first non-empathic environment—God/personal sin.

We are not suggesting that personal sin should be used as a weapon against people. Nor do we believe that people deserve to be violated because they are wretched sinners. On the contrary, every person should be treated with grace and compassion, especially when working through the layers of anger and pain associated with abuse.

The point is that the first and second non-empathic environments must be considered a unit. The sins committed against us must not be emphasized to the exclusion of personal sin. Both environments have profoundly influenced the people we are today. Both surroundings were unsafe, frightening places in which we knew, deep down, that something was terribly wrong with us and with our relationships.

When we do not deal with the ramifications of the first non-empathic environment, we get caught in the web of endless sin, misusing God's good tools. Boundaries actually become barriers as we seek to keep unsafe people away. We become an exclusive group of people rather than inclusive. Bonding with God is replaced by bonding with other people. Other than occasional lip service, God is often left completely out of the recovery process.[15] "Healing the inner child" and "taking care of myself for a change" become habitual opportunities to indulge in self-centered living.

Our personal sin against God, which disrupted all relationships, is the first cause of all our personality problems and must not be neglected in the recovery process. When we ignore our own sin, we can turn good tools into instruments of evil. Our tendency toward this kind of self-deception can be traced back to the threefold inner conflict we inherited from Adam and Eve (the first non-empathic environment). When we're not living in obedience to the Lord, our natural propensity toward pursuing our own godhood is very strong. Apart from Christ, we want to be a god. It is evident from the examples above that when recovery principles are misused in this way, the self is still enthroned.

When we come to grips with our sinful responses to the sins committed against us, we are less likely to pervert good concepts such as boundaries, bonding, and caring for oneself. Christ is able to help us use these tools for our healing and his glory.

The longer we walk in obedience to Christ, the more we will understand others as well as ourselves. We can learn to forgive, accept, and love our abusers. In time, he will redeem our past experiences and use them to transform us into his likeness. We will eventually grow to maturity in him. Though this is a painful process, the benefits, in this life and in the life to come, far outweigh the pain.[16]

8

The Process of Biblical Recovery

> Therefore if any man is in Christ, he is a new creature; the old things passed away; behold, new things have come.
>
> The apostle Paul
> 2 Corinthians 5:17

What Is the New Creation?

Many of us in recovery cringe when we read or hear the words "new creatures in Christ." The apostle Paul is proclaiming a profound and liberating truth, yet it is met with resentment and disillusionment by us, the people who need to hear it the most.

The reason we shrink from this glorious truth is quite simple: Many well-meaning fellow believers have applied Paul's words to our hurting situation in a way that leaves us feeling condemned. In order to console us in our time of suffering, believing friends and relatives bring us to 2 Corinthians 5:17.[1] They compassionately tell us this verse means that our past experiences are dead and gone. Our former lives should no longer affect us because we are now new creatures in Christ. Past feelings, memories, and problems should no longer have any hold on us.

These brothers and sisters in Christ are only trying to help us, but their interpretation of this text leaves us feeling more inadequate and guilty. We do still struggle with our past so we must be complete failures; we cannot seem to make God's Word work for us in this situation.

Does Paul really mean that our past experiences, feelings, and memories have passed away and no longer affect us? Thankfully, the overall context of this passage does not support the interpretation that they have been supernaturally blocked from our present awareness. It therefore cannot be applied to our lives in this manner. However, a proper understanding of this text must be applied to our lives so we eventually will be liberated from the tyranny of our past.

In 2 Corinthians 5:11–15, the apostle Paul, under the inspiration of the Holy Spirit, gives us keys to unlock the door to true freedom. In verse 11, he lays out his motivation for service, which is the "fear of the Lord." Because Christ is the ultimate judge (v. 10), Paul's reverent fear motivates him to preach the message of reconciliation (2 Cor. 5:16–6:2). Within this context the apostle speaks about the "new creature" (v. 17).

At the beginning of verse 17, the word "therefore" indicates that there is a logical connection between the present statement and the previous discussion. Hence, the key to understanding what the new creature is (as well as what has passed away) is found in verses 14–16. Christ died for all mankind. We should no longer live for ourselves, but for him who was raised from the dead (vv. 14–15). We should not view human beings from superficial, external appearances "according to the flesh" (i.e., attractiveness or nationality), even as we no longer view Christ as a mere man (v. 16). We should consider fellow human beings from the perspective of their spiritual status, whether they are in Christ or not (v. 17). The one in Christ is a new creation supernaturally engaging in Christ-centered (truthful) living.

In other words, new creatures in Christ no longer live for themselves, pursuing what they want to be (ultimately, equal to God—the first non-empathic environment). What has passed away is self-centered living (v. 15), not past experiences, feelings, and memories. We were not given an eternal case of amnesia when we entered into this new life. We were given a new motivation for living—for Christ. The sinful nature, bent on rebelling against God and driven toward self-indulgence, is what has passed away in Christ.

The focus of 2 Corinthians 5:14–6:2 is Christ. Paul is controlled by the love of Christ (v. 14). Believers should live for Christ and not for themselves because he died and rose again (v. 15). We should view human beings from a spiritual standpoint because we now know Christ in a spiritual way (v. 16). We are new creatures in Christ, our self-centered way of living having passed away in him (v. 17). We are reconciled to God in Christ (vv. 18–19). Paul is an ambassador for Christ (v. 20). We become the righteousness of God in Christ (v. 21). Paul is working together with Christ to proclaim "the day of salvation" (2 Cor. 6:1–2).

Christ *is* the life of believers (Col. 3:2). He gives us a new identity and a new motivation for living. While it cannot be directly deduced from this passage (2 Cor. 5:14–6:2), other portions of Scripture support the fact that Christ causes us to respond to our hurtful past in a godly manner.[2] Through the process of sanctification, forgiveness and genuine love will begin to characterize our lives.

The Only True Candidate for Biblical Recovery

While well-meaning believers, who desperately want to help, may misinterpret the meaning of the new creature, many recovery proponents disregard this fundamental truth of our new identity in Christ altogether. In the name of common grace,[3] the distinction between the believer and the unbeliever is completely blurred.

But not to consider the vast spiritual difference between the Christian and non-Christian is to undermine the majority of foundational teachings found in the New Testament. The Pauline epistles, for example, consistently distinguish between believers and unbelievers. Let us briefly examine the substantial difference between the believer and the unbeliever.

Recovering believers are justified; therefore, they are a forgiven people who have been given a new identity in Christ. They are children of God who live in the light and who are actually of the light. Having been empowered by the Holy Spirit, they are no longer controlled by sin. They have a brand-new motivation for living and a future filled with hope. Believers are also assured of the ultimate happy ending—an eternal recovery.[4]

Recovering *un*believers, on the other hand, cannot claim any of these heavenly treasures. God has certainly offered his precious gift of salvation to every human being, but his salvation must be accepted into one's life for it to be effective. Hence, because unbelievers have not appropriated God's saving grace, they lack the inner power to truly change at the core of their being. They also do not have the hope of an eternal recovery.

Inasmuch as unbelievers follow biblical principles such as forgiveness, confession, and honesty, they can achieve a certain amount of recovery. They might even find true, meaningful happiness in their human relationships. However, their recovery can only be partial because they have not been reconciled to God. They still suffer the repercussions of the first non-empathic environment (alienation, shame and guilt, the threefold conflict in the personality).

In examining 2 Corinthians further, we find that Paul dealt specifically with the issue of believers and unbelievers. He brought out the stark difference between them with these words:

> Do not be bound together with unbelievers; for what partnership have righteousness and lawlessness, or what fellowship has light with darkness? Or what harmony has Christ with Belial, or what has a believer in common with an unbeliever? Or what agreement has the temple of God with idols? For we are the temple of the living God; just as God said, "I will dwell in them

and walk among them; and I will be their God, and they shall be My people."

2 Corinthians 6:14–16

It is not absolutely clear from the context of this passage what kind of association the Corinthian church had with unbelievers. It is quite likely that they were marrying them or entering into business relationships with them. Whatever their relationship, the timeless principle revealed in this portion of Scripture is certainly applicable to us today.

We are the temple of the living God (1 Cor. 3:16). Unbelievers are not. God dwells in us, and we can walk with him (Eph. 4–5). He does not have this close relationship with unbelievers. In light of our new identity and our association with him, we are to be separate from unbelievers in our behaviors and attitudes, perfecting holiness out of reverence for God (2 Cor. 6:17–7:1).

There is also a spiritually qualitative difference between the believer and unbeliever. Recovery proponents who bypass this fundamental truth by not properly acknowledging this difference can actually promote further identity problems in both the saved and the unsaved. The saved are in Christ; the unsaved are still in Adam (Rom. 5:12–21). One is capable of healthy, God-centered growth; the other is not. One is spiritually alive; the other is spiritually dead.

The point is that only the believer can achieve biblical recovery, which encompasses the healing of both the spiritual and emotional. To treat the believer and unbeliever alike in terms of their spiritual recovery is to overlook essential parts of God's revelation concerning them. Their true identities are hidden behind a mass of psychological jargon.

Both Christians and non-Christians can accurately be labeled "dysfunctional adult-children from dysfunctional families." But there is a deeper level of spiritual truth about these two groups that must not be neglected in the recovery process; namely, believers are in Christ and unbelievers are spiritual outsiders (Col. 4:5). This fact alone radically affects one's motivation in seeking recovery, and it affects the overall outcome of the recovery process as well.

This crucial aspect of spiritual identity must be clarified, emphasized, and practically applied throughout the recovery process. Otherwise, believers will not fully experience the abundant blessings, strength, and healing that come from being rightly related to God. Conversely, unbelievers will not recognize their desperate need for salvation, nor will they experience the freedom to be obtained by steadfast obedience to God.

In the following sections, we will explore the various aspects of salvation and how they relate specifically to recovery. We will examine what took place in us at the time of conversion (who we are in Christ) and sanctification (how we mature in this new life). The work Christ accomplished for us on the cross has eternal benefits that profoundly impact our present-day life in this earthly realm. Salvation and sanctification are God's methods for bringing about spiritual and emotional recovery.

Salvation and Recovery

Through the gift of salvation, God offers us infinitely more than an eternal home in heaven. His life, dwelling in us today, empowers us to be the people of God, a maturing and godly community growing into the likeness of his Son. His love, grace, and mercy are present realities we can experience in the process of recovery. God enables us to face the truth about ourselves and our past and helps us integrate our new spiritual identity into our present lives.[5]

We are in Christ. The consequences of the first non-empathic environment (personal sin) have been swallowed up by his death and resurrection. We have been reconciled to God. Our personalities are radically transformed at the point of our conversion. In Christ, we begin to shed the false, idealized image of ourselves (our pursuit of godhood), and we gradually grow into what we were intended to be—a godly people growing in our unique abilities. Though it takes time to experience this reality, the innate shame and guilt we inherited from Adam is also removed in Christ.

Our calling, conversion, regeneration, justification, adoption, and glorification were acts preordained by God. They are the foundation of our new lives. We must integrate these divine truths into our recovery experience.

Let us now explore the specific aspects of salvation which relate to who we are in Christ.

Calling and Election

Long before time, God chose us to be his own. Before he laid the foundations of the world, we existed in his mind (Eph. 1:3–14). Acts 17:26 tells us that "he made from one, every nation of mankind to live on all the face of the earth, having determined their appointed times, and the boundaries of their habitation."

God did this so we would seek him and reach out for him. Even before we were saved he was not far from each one of us (Acts 17:27). We can safely deduce from this passage that he placed each of us in our specific families of origin. It was no accident that we had the parents we did or we were raised in our particular situation. God was well aware of our circumstances.

Because of our backgrounds and the associated pain, these doctrines of God's sovereignty, calling, and election could cause us to become bitter and angry toward him. (In fact, many people are presently struggling with these feelings.) But these teachings can also become a great source of joy and comfort. God has chosen us to be a part of his eternal plan, and he has worked in our lives to cause us to come to him. He has allowed various situations and circumstances to take place in order to bring us to the realization we need him. Ultimately, the doctrine of election assures us that we are secure with him, and his purpose for us will be brought to fruition.

God's sovereignty, calling, and election offer us the security many of us lacked in our families of origin. They are a guarantee that we will always be wanted and welcome. His eternal choice in electing us means that we will never be forsaken, no matter what we're going through.

It is difficult for many of us to experience these truths in our daily living, especially when we've known only rejection from those who were supposed to love us. However, as we meditate on those Scriptures that speak of our calling and election, God will impress these life-giving realities into our hearts forever.

Conversion

Dead human beings cannot be reformed; they can only be resurrected. Only life, Christ's life, can resuscitate and heal the human soul. When we said yes to God, we died to our old way of living; but we gained a brand-new life.

The apostle Paul says that we were actually dead in the sins which characterized our former way of life (Eph. 2:1–3). What we truly lost was our existence as the living dead. This is a loss not to be grieved, but to be celebrated. It is an existence that is qualitatively different from the old one. We entered into a new relationship with God, and he has given us the capacity to relate to ourselves and others in a healthy, Christlike manner.

This new life in Christ gives us hope. We have the hope that we are truly a changed people. This new beginning is filled with endless, God-centered possibilities. The Lord has bestowed upon us a new heart and a new mind so we may begin to think, will, and act in accordance with his new life in us.

Hope is an essential part of the recovery process. Through hope, we can view our past experiences from a new perspective, knowing that the present and the future will be different because we are different. In time, we will be able to respond to the people who hurt us out of the love and forgiveness that flow from our new life in Christ.

Regeneration

In his letter to Titus, Paul instructs the young pastor to remind his people to be submissive to authorities, to do good, to be gentle, and to show consideration to all men (Titus 3:1–2).

Then he gives the reason God's people should behave in this way: We were once like the disobedient. "For we also once were foolish ourselves, disobedient, deceived, enslaved to various lusts and pleasures, spending our life in malice and envy, hateful, hating one another" (Titus 3:3).

But these behaviors do not characterize the life of the believer anymore. Out of his kindness and mercy, God has saved us from this empty way of life. Christ redeemed us from this wickedness and purified us in order to make for himself a people who are his very own, eager to do what is good (Titus 2:14). It was not because of our righteous deeds that he saved us, "but according to His mercy, by the washing of *regeneration* and renewing by the Holy Spirit, whom He poured out upon us richly through Jesus Christ our Savior" (Titus 3:5–6, italics ours).

Despite this glorious truth about regeneration, many are still "enslaved to various lusts and pleasures" (v. 3), obsessive/compulsive patterns, and are still struggling with hatefulness. Because we are not yet willing to face our pain, we hide behind these sinful behaviors. However, the doctrine of regeneration assures us that God has given us the power to change.

The new life we received at the time of our conversion not only fills us with hope, it endues us with the power to change through the Holy Spirit. We do not break sinful habits by willpower but through obedience to the Holy Spirit, who gives us a new heart and fills us with God-centered desires. Although this new heart is given to us at conversion, it takes time to experience these spiritual benefits.

The Holy Spirit, through the process of sanctification, gradually enables us to live in accordance with this new nature. We soon lose the desire to live contrary to God's will. The doctrine of regeneration means that we have the power to change through the Holy Spirit. God has not left us alone to fight the battles against our sinful behaviors.

Justification

In Romans 4, Paul shows that Abraham, an example to all believers, was justified and considered righteous because he believed in the promises of God. His life provides a testimony to those who must follow in his footsteps of faith.

"Therefore having been justified by faith, we have peace with God through our Lord Jesus Christ" (Rom. 5:1). The hostility that once existed between God and human beings is destroyed through Jesus Christ. The first non-empathic environment (God/personal sin) resulting from Adam's disobedience is healed. Believers now enjoy a relationship of peace and tranquility with their Creator.

Justification is a legal term. Through the act of justification, God pardons sinners who place their faith in Jesus Christ. He declares them righteous and blameless. Consequently, believers will not suffer the penalty of their sin because they are no longer under God's wrath. Jesus Christ paid off their eternal debt in full by his death and resurrection.

Therefore, the doctrine of justification means that we are free from the innate shame and guilt inherited from Adam and Eve. There is "no condemnation for those who are in Christ Jesus" (Rom. 8:1) because he has set us free from the consequences of our sin. He banished the shame and guilt that once kept us from him, and we can now live our lives in his presence.

However, shame and guilt still haunt those who were consistently told at earlier stages of life that they were bad. Many were treated like damaged merchandise in their families of origin. Therefore, they find it hard to believe that God could love or want people like them. After all, if their own families shamed them and thought they were a mistake, how can they believe that God could really accept them and remove their disgrace?

Yet those in recovery can believe that God accepts them because his Word is a trustworthy testimony to this marvelous truth. As with other aspects of salvation, it takes time to experience the reality of this imputed righteousness in daily life. Nevertheless, the shame and guilt acquired from the second non-empathic environment (human relationships/being sinned against) will gradually fade away as their minds are renewed in Christ and as they engage in healthy relationships.

Adoption

Romans 8 speaks predominantly about our spiritual life in Christ. In it Paul boldly declares our new status as children of God. He says that we "have not received a spirit of slavery leading to fear again, but [we] have received a spirit of adoption as sons by which we cry out 'Abba! Father!'" (Rom. 8:15).

Paul also weaves this adoption theme throughout his discussion of the Law in the Book of Galatians. Christ redeemed those under the Law that they might receive adoption as God's children (Gal. 4:5). Again, he writes that "because (we) are sons, God has sent forth the Spirit of His Son into our hearts, crying, 'Abba! Father!'" (Gal. 4:6).

It is Christ who has given us the authority to become children of God (John 1:12). He reconciled us to God, liberated us from bondage to sin, gave us a new identity in him, made us coheirs of his kingdom, and ushered us into a new spiritual family. We are under the Father's loving care because he wanted us. Jesus, his Son, made this Father/child relationship possible.

The doctrine of adoption assures us that we are wanted and we belong. This is a life-giving truth for those who have felt unwanted and rejected all of their lives. Our new status as God's children cannot be revoked because it is sealed in Christ's blood. Our earthly parents may not have given us any confirmation that we are valuable. But God gave his only Son to prove that he loved us by making us his own.

In other words, the cross of Christ means that God has committed himself to us forever. We belong to him and to each other as members of his family.[6] King David said in Psalm 27:10 that his father and mother had forsaken him, but the Lord would receive him. We must embrace this truth as David did in order to experience God's comfort through our recovery process.

Glorification

"Whom He predestined, these He also called; and whom He called, these He also justified; and whom He justified, these He also glorified" (Rom. 8:30). Glorification is the completion of God's work in salvation. At the time of our conversion, we are given a new heart, our spirit is made alive, we are freed from bondage to sin, and we are justified and adopted into the family of God.

Glorification is the redemption of our bodies. The sinful nature is finally shed and no longer holds any influence on us. At the time of the rapture of the church,[7] we will be given glorified bodies, similar to Jesus' resurrected body. The second coming of Christ will not only bring human salvation to completion, it will ultimately culminate in the renewal of all creation.[8]

In that day, God will create a new heaven and a new earth. Our present existence will pass away.

> And I saw a new heaven and a new earth; for the first heaven and the first earth passed away, and there is no longer any sea. And I heard a loud voice from the throne, saying, "Behold, the tabernacle of God is among men, and He shall dwell among them, and they shall be His people, and God Himself shall be among them, and He shall wipe away every tear from their eyes; and there shall no longer be any death; there shall no longer be any mourning, or crying, or pain; the first things have passed away." And He who sits on the throne said, "Behold, I am making all things new."
>
> Revelation 21:1, 3–5

The doctrine of glorification means the promise of eternal recovery. Believers in Christ are guaranteed complete healing. One day we will enter into an existence that is free from pain and suffering, where God himself will dwell visibly with his people. Glorification is the culmination of God's work in salvation. We face overwhelming difficulties in this world, but God's purposes for his people shall prevail. He has promised us that our mourning will ultimately be turned to joy.

All of these aspects of salvation are the result of God's working in our lives. It was his purpose and pleasure to save us from our miserable existence in Adam. By his grace we are in Christ, we receive a new identity in him, and we are given a new motivation to live for him.

However, there is another side to the salvation experience in which we respond to what God has done in our lives. This is known as sanctification. In the sanctification process, we respond to God's Spirit in order to grow to maturity in Christ. Let us now explore this topic and how it relates to recovery.

Sanctification and Recovery

As we were saved by God's grace, so are we sanctified by his grace.[9] God's Spirit is at work in us to move us toward holy living, but we must cooperate with his leading and submit ourselves to his will. We are able to respond to God's will because he has made us new creatures in Christ. His seed has been planted in us to enable us to walk as Jesus did (1 John 3:9).

Unlike the aspects of salvation mentioned in the previous section, sanctification is not instantaneously bestowed upon us at the time of conversion. It is a growth process. We grow to maturity in Christ as we live in obedience to him. The basic ability to obey God is given to us the moment we place our faith in Christ; but it takes time to produce the fruit of this new life.

While the goal of sanctification is the same for every believer (growing into Christlikeness), the process of sanctification is significantly different for each individual. Some people easily submit to the Lord's will from the beginning and quickly build a trusting relationship with him; others, finding it difficult to trust, struggle in their relationship with God. They cannot readily experience his love or presence in their daily lives.

Many in recovery fall into the latter category of believers. They want to trust God but falter in their faith. They feel inadequate because they cannot experience the Lord's love the way other believers do. They are often treated like second-class Christians because they struggle with these issues.

These are special problems facing those who have experienced the second non-empathic environment. The continual exposure to physical and/or emotional abuse and mistreatment has robbed many of a normal ability to trust and relate to others. They carry unresolved pain and anger from these experiences, and these interfere with their present relationships.

Obviously, not every believer has relational problems of this magnitude. Those who do have a difficult time trusting and relating to God and others need specialized sanctification in Christ. Through the Recovery Movement, God has graciously provided the church with tools to help people who grapple with these relational issues.

As we discussed in the previous chapter, these recovery tools have often been used as instruments of evil by those in the church who have not been willing to deal with their personal sin (harboring anger and unforgiveness). Recovery principles have also been abused by those who teach them to hurting believers. Let us briefly discuss the mishandling of these tools by authorities as it relates to the process of sanctification.

God's goal for every Christian in the sanctifying process is not simply to grow, but to grow in Christ. We are to mature in Christ because he perfectly manifests the image of God and flawlessly reflects what human beings were originally intended to be. There are certain precepts we are commanded to follow in order to move us toward the goal of maturity in Christ: prayer, confession of sin, repentance, and obedience.[10]

In an attempt to meet the felt needs of people who are struggling in their earthly relationships, Christian self-help programs primarily utilize recovery tools such as formulating boundaries, bonding with others, and inner healing. These same recovery programs seem to bypass the real need of distraught believers by neglecting to emphasize the importance of obeying God's commands in the sanctification process.

We must fully recognize that God's Word is our ultimate authority. Truthful living forces us to be honest with ourselves, but more importantly, it requires us to be obedient to the will of God. We must practice legitimate, biblical recovery principles without abandoning God's commands to pray, confess sin, repent, and obey him. Recovery techniques and God's truth must be balanced in the Christian's life.

Unfortunately, it is commonly argued in these same recovery circles that obedience to the Lord is not possible until we have achieved some level of spiritual growth. This is like putting the cart before the horse. While it is true that we will consistently falter in our obedience to him until we have reached a certain degree of spiritual maturity, it is not impossible for an immature believer to obey God.

The basic assumption that holds that someone is not able to obey the Lord or make right choices until he is spiritually mature is simply not biblical. In fact, the Scriptures support the opposite view: We must obey God in order to grow spiritually.

This is the logic behind Jesus' teaching to his disciples in the upper room (John 14–15). The night before his crucifixion, as he was eating his last Passover meal, Jesus commanded his disciples to abide in him and to obey his commandments. Then they would bear much fruit for him. There is no indication in Jesus' teaching that the apostles could not abide in him or obey him until they became spiritually mature. Obedience would result in their spiritual growth. They would be able to live fruitful lives for him because spiritual fruit flows from an obedient life.

The apostles reiterate this theme of obedience throughout their letters.[11] We grow in our ability to obey God as we mature in Christ. Obedience is essential for spiritual growth and healing in the biblical recovery process.

As recovering believers, we must understand that God's goal for our lives is not simply to make us healthy but holy. Healthiness is the natural outcome of an obedient life. God loves us and deeply cares about the difficulties we have in our relationships with him and others. This is why he wants us to lead a committed life. He knows that obedience is the only way we will grow spiritually and develop our relational abilities.[12]

Therefore, our aim as Christians should not be happiness but holiness. Herein lies true joy and freedom. And we can utterly rely on the Holy Spirit to give us the power and wisdom to pursue this kind of life.

In figure 8.1 you will find "A Biblical Creed for Christians in Recovery." It contains the various aspects of salvation and sanc-

128

Fig. 8.1

A Biblical Creed for Christians in Recovery

I am a new creature in Christ. I have a new identity through faith in him. I am no longer a shamed and guilt-ridden person. By God's grace and out of his great love for me, he gave me new life through his gift of salvation.

This is what God has done for me:

Calling and election: I have been chosen before the world began. He has given me eternal *security* (Eph. 1:3–14).

Conversion: I have been given new life in Christ. He has given me *hope* and a *new beginning* (1 Peter 1:22–25).

Regeneration: I have been made spiritually alive. He has given me his Holy Spirit and *the power to change* (Titus 3:5–6).

Justification: I have been pardoned from my sin and declared righteous in his sight. He has given me *freedom from shame and guilt* (Rom. 5:1; Rom. 8:1).

Adoption: I have been adopted into God's family. I am *wanted* and I *belong* to him (Rom. 8:15–16).

Glorification: I will dwell in the presence of God in the new heaven and new earth for eternity. I will receive a glorified body. He has given me *the promise of eternal recovery* (Rev. 21:1–5).

Through the power of the Holy Spirit, I will live in accordance with who I am in Christ. My life will be characterized by:

Prayer: I will reverently seek God in prayer. I will be *honest* with him and myself about the pain and problems in my life (Rom. 12:12).

Confession: I will confess my sin to the Lord and to my brothers and sisters in Christ. I will admit *my need for help and healing* (2 John 1:9).

Fig. 8.1

A Biblical Creed for Christians in Recovery
(continued)

Repentance: By God's grace and through the power of his Spirit, I will work to change my sinful behaviors. I will learn to walk by faith in his promises (Rev. 2:5; 3:3).

Obedience: Through the help of God's Spirit, I will live my life according to his will. I will be a committed disciple of Jesus Christ (1 John 2:4–5).

tification discussed in this chapter along with their timeless recovery principles.

Meditate on these truths several times during the day. God will begin to transform your mind so that you may see yourself for who you really are—a new creature in Christ. You are a person who has already received abundant blessings through God's gracious gift of salvation. You can achieve substantial transformation of your emotional and behavioral patterns in the power of the Holy Spirit, through obedience to the Lord of Recovery.

9

The Unseen Conflict

> While we may be firmly grounded in sound doctrine and accept our responsibility to live a godly life, we need to be aware of the fierce invisible warfare being waged against us. . . . The forces arrayed against us are powerful, but the weapons God gives us are adequate for our defense.
>
> *Life Recovery Bible*
> Notes on Ephesians 6:10–13

NOW THAT THE Cold War has wound down the American CIA and the Russian KGB may eventually release accounts of some of their undercover operations. If that happens, there will undoubtedly be records of situations in which both agencies had operatives hidden in some of the most delicate and well-secured incidents of the last generation.

The armies of spirit beings loyal to God and Satan are like these organizations and their covert involvement in high-stakes and almost invisible situations. Though none were ever seen, Jesus assured his followers that he could summon "more than twelve legions of angels" to his side in the Garden of Gethsemane (Matt. 26:53). Paul, on the other hand, warned his readers that "our struggle is not against flesh and blood, but against the rulers, against the powers, against the world forces of this darkness" (Eph. 6:12).

So, we find ourselves in the middle of a war zone where an unseen conflict is swirling all around us. There is no possibility of truce. The warfare will rage until Satan is finally seized and confined by the Lord's forces (Rev. 20).

Make no mistake, Christians are not like the citizens of Switzerland, who declared themselves neutral and largely stayed out of World Wars I and II as the battle engulfed Europe. Believers are involved in this spiritual warfare, whether they like it or not. In fact, the devil intends to overwhelm Christians who are not alert to such matters much as a lion devours its prey (1 Peter 5:8). Accordingly, God has dispatched angels to serve and protect his people (Heb. 1:14).

The focal questions for this chapter are: (1) What does spiritual warfare have to do with recovery?; and (2) How can an awareness of spiritual warfare enhance full-scale spiritual recovery?

Angelology: The Intersection of Spiritual Warfare and Spiritual Recovery

Much of church history has been preoccupied with the origins of angels and demons,[1] even to such trivialities as how many angelic beings can fit on the head of a needle. Only in recent times have theology and ministry begun to work with angelology in a practical manner. Yet, even today it is not uncommon for evangelical general theological survey works to overlook angelology.[2] However, since 1987–88 and the beginning of the evangelical Recovery Movement, a connection between angelology and recovery issues has begun to be drawn.[3] Thus, the interface between the fields is very much a frontier in the early stages of being settled.

There can be little doubt that there is a strong connection. The relationship is clearcut wherever biblical characters caught up in spiritual warfare are seen with recognizable recovery issues.[4] For example, many of the people Jesus healed entered the spotlight of the biblical narrative out of painful personal, family backgrounds related to demonic influence (e.g., Matt. 17:14–18). Some of these people went on to play significant ministry roles in the New Testament, including Mary Magdalene (Luke 8:2) as well as the slave girl in Philippi (Acts 16:16–18), who apparently became one of the early members of the Philippian church (if the natural implication is drawn from discussing her story between the stones of Lydia and the Philippian jailer).

Demonstrating that spiritual warfare and recovery are related biblically and practically is not difficult. They intersect like two superhighways running through Scripture. Because of this, we must carefully study the Scriptures for implications regarding evangelical recovery treatment today.

First, we will probe into three classic examples of spiritual warfare in the Old Testament: Adam and Eve, Job, and King Saul. Next, after implications are drawn for the study of parapsychology, principles from several related New Testament passages will be compiled for application in realistic spiritual recovery warfare. Finally, a "bottom-line" biblical-theological perspective on demonic influence and recovery will be offered.

Spiritual Warfare in Scripture

Adam and Eve

Recovery can be defined simply as "the comeback process from an unhealthy event, relationship, or behavioral pattern that continues to impact a person's life in negative ways."[5] If such a viewpoint is legitimate, then Adam's and Eve's sin was, literally, the foundational unhealthy event of human history, the first fallen domino to start the chain reaction of behavioral and relational dominoes ever since (i.e., the first non-empathic environment).[6]

Spiritual warfare was central to the tragic outworking of the incident. The New Testament makes it clear that the serpent in Genesis 3 was the puppet of the devil (Rev. 12:9). The serpent's subtle distortion of the truth in the initial scene (Gen.

3:4–5), followed by the unwillingness of Adam and Eve to accept responsibility for their sinful actions (vv. 10–13), brought about the horrible long-term consequences of the curses in verses 14–19. This brought Adam and Eve to the point of hitting bottom (including losing their home in the Garden of Eden in verses 22–24), a point that often constitutes the starting point of recovery.

However, Adam and Eve had not learned all the lessons about the consequences of their sin. Their oldest son, Cain, killed their younger son, Abel, and, as Adam and Eve had done in the Garden, Cain tried to lie about it to God (Gen. 4:9–10). As a result, Cain bore the terrible consequences of his sin (vv. 11–15) and chose to turn his back on God (v. 16).

Things did get started back in the right direction of godly recovery with the next son, Seth (Gen. 4:25–26). But what a mess the human race had already become by this second generation! And, it had all started with the father and mother of us all naively falling prey to spiritual warfare.[7]

Job's Trauma

The events in Job 1–2 move the spiritual warfare seen in the Old Testament into the unseen realm. Though readers of the biblical narrative are keenly aware of the repeated interaction between God and Satan (Job 1:6–12; 2:1–6), there is no indication that Job himself had even the first clue about the satanic assault while it was going on.[8]

Besides getting across how dangerous unawareness can be, Job's situation also demonstrates the natural tendency to explain whatever tragedies happen in the life of a believer in terms of sin alone (Job 1:1, 8, 22). While Job eventually repents of his proud anger (Job 32:1; 42:1–6), his part-time comforters are the objects of God's anger because they foolishly undertook a directive counseling approach (i.e., assuming Job's sinfulness) without having any idea beyond surface appearances as to what was really happening (Job 4–31).[9]

It becomes readily apparent from the Book of Job that a full-orbed theological approach to recovery requires looking at more than just the sins of the fathers and personal sin and dysfunction. If the unseen—but equally real—spiritual warfare element is left out, the tragedies and problems overwhelming the lives of many godly people may be squeezed into the reductionistic mold of many modern Job-type comforters.

An "Out-of-Bounds" Counseling Session

Another classic Old Testament example in which the recovery grid and spiritual warfare intersect is King Saul's counseling session with the witch of Endor, recorded in 1 Samuel 28. The saddest part of this entire incident is that when Saul's problems multiplied, he hypocritically convinced himself that his immediate need for counsel (vv. 3–7) justified going "out of bounds" for help.

In seeking insight from beyond the grave (v. 11), Saul had been seduced by the spiritism existing in the environment in Canaan in that day (v. 9). Scripture clearly prohibits God's people from pursuing such sources (Deut. 18:9–13), a fact Saul knew very well (1 Sam. 28:9). But he thought it was the only way he could get his questions answered (v. 15) and, undeniably, it worked.

Unfortunately, many Christians—both counselors and counselees—have apparently followed in the footsteps of this confused and pathetic king of Israel. When "whatever works" becomes the primary reason one either does therapy in a certain way or seeks help from a certain counselor, without strong consideration of the biblical-theological ramifications involved, he is courting disaster, as Saul found out (1 Sam. 28:15–19). The point is this: The evangelicals' idea of effectiveness of treatment in recovery must never be allowed to sink to the level of "whatever works."

Even though the criticisms of certain recovery treatment approaches (like visualization) paint everything with the broadest of brushstrokes, there are instances in which such critics are on target. We are aware of cases, even in a few evangelical, church-based support groups, in which, knowingly or not, New Age/occult techniques have been employed. It is widely admitted by evangelicals that participation in New Age, and especially occult, practices is a frequent doorway to demonic influence in believers' lives. Therefore, everyone involved in the recovery counseling process would do well to stay as far away as possible from any possible "out of bounds" concepts or techniques, no matter how well they work. There is already enough spiritual warfare swirling around Christian recovery without asking for it by employing questionable approaches.

Anchoring Parapsychology in Scripture

The closest category that the systematized study of psychology has to offer to the focus of this chapter is parapsychology. Since naturalistic secular psychology is largely still in denial about the reality of the supernatural and the unseen spiritual realm, parapsychology is a maverick science at best. Yet, with the recent (often high-profile) proliferation of psychics in our society, as well as more and more claims of occult or satanic ritual abuse, it is clearly a needed subdiscipline of psychology.[10]

The connection here is that parapsychology can be little more than a sensationalized descriptive discipline (i.e., limited to observing what happens) without a clear moral compass. But, the stakes are much too high for Christians, who counsel those who have been involved in the paranormal, to rely on just a basic sense of right and wrong or even an occasional biblical proof-text.

Surely the time has come in which a theologically validated study of parapsychology is needed. Without such a distinctive functioning discipline, operating with clearly evangelical assumptions, the wider field of parapsychology will be left to dabble dangerously in the supernatural. Also, without such a specialized field, the study and practice of psychology by evangelicals leaves itself wide open to accusations either of overlooking or ignoring an area of need[11] or worse, merely parroting the typically naturalistic secular agenda for psychology.

It is fruitless to argue that these needed changes cannot be brought about quickly and decisively in evangelical psychology and recovery counseling. Drastic rapid changes in allowable insurance coverage are forcing most evangelical counseling organizations to scramble full-speed to find new ways to offer treatment, and they are doing it because it is directly related to their financial bottom line. The haunting question here is: Are the twin commitments to biblical authority and the mushrooming needs of the society in which they practice "bottom line" enough to prompt evangelical psychological professionals to get their acts together in the emerging arena of parapsychology/spiritual warfare?

A "Bottom Line" Approach

Lingering Anger: Allowing a Devilish Foothold

Ephesians 4:26–27 is frequently handled as a spiritual warfare passage in its caution about the devil getting a foot in the door through a believer's lingering anger. These verses also have ramifications for counseling, even though the person seeking counseling or intensive therapy has usually already let the anger and bitterness (v. 31) simmer in the emotional oven for considerably longer than a sundown (v. 26).

What happens when you consider anger and spiritual warfare side by side? If lingering anger is the foyer through which much first-stage spiritual warfare enters and numerous counseling problems heat up emotionally, they would seem almost inseparable. Perhaps it is indeed more accurate to view this anger-rooted spiritual warfare and the anger-related counseling problems as interwoven. Just like it is not possible adequately to clean out a drainage pipe without dealing with the tree roots that have grown through it, there is futility in going after either the counseling problem or the root of the spiritual warfare alone. The answer is not either/or; it's both/and. When significant anger shows itself in a counseling situation, playing safe with the clearcut truth of Ephesians 4:26–27 requires seriously considering the inroads of demonic warfare in the troubled person's life.

Weapons for Spiritual Warfare and Recovery

It may seem that linking Ephesians 4:27 to full-blown spiritual warfare is stretching things a bit. However, the next place in the epistle where the devil is mentioned is in Ephesians 6:11, the foundational biblical passage for the spiritual armor the Lord provides to protect his people in the unseen warfare (vv. 10–18).[12]

The implication from theologically correlating these two passages is that anger is an example of a chink in believers' armor. If something as seemingly inconsequential as the failure to deal quickly with anger can present an opportunity for the devil, believers had better spiritually arm themselves to the teeth. This is especially true since the evil day when such armor is needed (v. 13) is not in the future or at some crisis point, but every day of life (Eph. 5:16).

It is almost certain Paul patterns his description of the spiritual armor after that worn by the Roman soldiers who were guarding him in jail (Eph. 3:1; 6:20). Most pieces of the armor play a primarily defensive part.[13] Spiritual attack by the devil's army of darkness (Eph. 6:12) is essentially spiritual guerrilla warfare, so only the "sword of the Spirit, which is the Word of God" (v. 17) and prayer (v. 18) are available as offensive weaponry.

This passage must also be carefully considered from the standpoint of recovery. Again, it is not an either/or choice between spiritual warfare and a recovery-related issue. Figure 9.1 visualizes how the two areas work together to enable the recovering Christian to stand firm against not only "the schemes of the devil" (Eph. 6:11) but also the world and the flesh.

True biblical recovery requires balance.[14] It is not possible to be fully balanced unless all three of these fronts (the demonic, the world, and the flesh) are covered. Recovery counseling can help establish useful boundaries, which can, in the power of the Holy Spirit (Gal. 5:22–23; Eph. 5:18),[15] help hold in check temptations related to the flesh and the world. But, it is the combination of the inner line of defense, provided by the armor of God, and the invisible outer perimeter defense, pro-

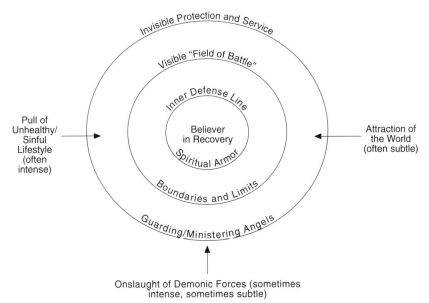

Fig. 9.1
**Personal Spiritual Warfare and Recovery:
Healthy Scriptural Lines of Defense**

vided by the angels the Lord assigns to protect his children (Heb.1:14), that keep the demonic forces in check and recovery on track.

You're in Good Hands Even Though You Can't See Them

In connection with the issues of biblical recovery and spiritual warfare, protection is paramount. It is a great comfort to recovering believers, who cannot see their angelic protectors, to hear with Elisha's servant, "Do not fear, for those who are with us are more than those who are with them" (2 Kings 6:16). There may be recovering believers who have a very hard time believing the Lord would really care enough to assign angels to them like personal bodyguards, but it is true. Even the "little ones" (Matt. 18:10), whether children (vv. 1–5) or spiritually immature believers, all have their own heavenly angels.

We can also be assured that the Lord will dispatch as many angels as necessary to meet the needs of his children. With Peter, it was only one (Acts 12:7–11). With Daniel, there were two, one of whom was Michael, the archangel (Dan. 10:12–14). With Jesus, it was several after his temptation (Matt. 4:11), and could have been many thousands in the Garden of Gethsemane had they been needed (Matt. 26:53). Part of the wonder of God's protection for us through his angels is that there will always be enough to keep us safe, according to his will.

Overcoming and Suffering

On his first missionary journey, the apostle Paul teaches the new disciples that "through many tribulations we must enter the kingdom of God" (Acts 14:22). This is a complementary point to the unseen reality of guardian angels. Believers are protected (Heb. 1:14), but they should not consider it strange or out of character to suffer (1 Peter 4:12). The Lord utilizes such suffering as the testing procedure to bring about endurance and maturity (James 1:3–4).

This does not mean that all suffer the same amount. Just as there was no explanation for why Job suffered more than those around him, no single biblical explanation is given to those recovering believers who are allowed to suffer more than other Christians.

However, there is at least one significant reason attached to the recovery process itself that explains additional suffering. Being a consistent overcomer attracts satanic attention like a lightning rod. This is seen most clearly in the letters to the seven churches in Revelation 2–3. Of the seven, four were experiencing tremendous attacks of spiritual warfare: the churches at Sardis, Pergamum, Thyatira, and Philadelphia. The mini-letters to each of these particular churches clearly refer to Satan or his human henchmen (Rev. 2:9, 13, 24; 3:9).

Why were these Christians having trouble with the devil while the other three churches were not? Apparently it was because the individual believers in each of these four churches were consistently living as overcomers, as the Lord said at the end of each of their letters, and this infuriated the devil! On the other hand, the Lord described the other three churches, none of which were experiencing any difficulty, as fallen (Rev. 2:5), spiritually dead (Rev. 3:1), and lukewarm (Rev. 3:16). They posed no threat to Satan and his agenda, so he left them alone.

These Scriptures illustrate that those who are overcomers, whether generally or through biblical recovery, can expect to have it tougher than professing, non-practicing Christians who are simply going through the motions or heavily in denial. However, when the going gets tough, an overcomer's growth accelerates. For those in recovery, hard times cause growth spurts toward the kind of consistency and stability never known before, and the suffering ends up being worth its weight in gold.

Demonic Influence and Possession

To specifically discuss dealing with those who, because of spiritual warfare, are demonized is a more complex subject than this type of study allows. Still, such a discussion requires some answer to the question: "Can a believer in Jesus Christ be possessed by a demon?" Those who answer this question with "No!" usually appeal to the believer's security and to 1 John 4:4: "Greater is He who is in you than he who is in the world." The reasoning behind this view is that, because God (or the Holy Spirit) indwelling the believer is greater, he cannot be displaced or overwhelmed by the devil, "the god of this world" (2 Cor. 4:4). Those who answer "Yes!" generally rely upon the free will of the believer to choose, even in a direction with strong demonic activity. They disagree with the above interpretation of 1 John 4:4, partly because 1 John 4:3, the previous verse, speaks not of Satan but of the antichrist.

There is also a persistent squabble over terminology. The commonly used terms "possession," "oppression," and "influence" sound precise enough to be helpful. But definitions vary, and there is no consensus. Therefore, it becomes an even more complex debate.

Finally, there is the input of various deliverance practitioners and others who have dealt with demonized people. Their experience is, of course, very useful because it moves beyond disputed theory and theology. However, reliance on experience alone promotes the danger of reducing truth to the oft-heard pragmatism of "whatever works."

At this juncture, it seems fair to say that none of the competing perspectives has a lock on the question of demon possession of Christians. Perhaps, in light of the healing nature of recovery and the slippery, powerful nature of spiritual warfare, it is high time to try to move beyond the impasse. The best way to do this would be a "bottom line," biblical-practical approach.

Such an approach would need to begin with this realistic biblical perspective: In looking at the lives of people, we cannot use "hasty judgments"[16] to declare whether someone is a Christian, especially when something like demonic activity is involved. According to the parable of the wheat and the tares (Matt. 13:24–30, 36–43), "at the judgment men's true condition is brought to light, and genuine believers are separated from the spurious."[17]

Realizing that the principle, "Man looks at the outward appearance, but the LORD looks at the heart" (1 Sam. 16:7), is true even in spiritual warfare is a crucial biblical bridge to practical action. It is largely futile to finally determine whether a demonized person is a Christian,[18] most of the force of the original question evaporates. What remains is to be better safe than sorry by compassionately attempting to help the person be released from the demonic power that has invaded his or her life. In such a case, it is better to assume a worst case scenario than to underestimate the strength of the demonic hold and not help the person find release. It is also very important to make sure that, if the demon leaves, the vacuum within is filled by Jesus Christ through faith. Not doing so risks setting the person up for future demonic attack, where "the last state of that man becomes worse than the first" (Matt. 12:45).

This viable, biblical, and workable angle for dealing with those who are demonized is to first, wisely assume nothing decisive about the person's eternal destiny during the process of casting out the demon; and, second, compassionately do everything possible to offer decisive biblical and spiritual resources to the person formerly controlled by the demon. The release will only be permanent if there is a decisive shift in the controlling power to the Holy Spirit (Eph. 5:18).

The offer and availability of such biblical-practical considerations may be what makes all the difference in whether a person will enter (or reenter) the full biblical recovery process. If it turns out the formerly demonized person was a non-Christian, this approach makes a life and death difference, if he or she takes the first step of biblical recovery through saving faith. But even if it turns out that the demonically-controlled person was a Christian, having fallen (or relapsed) in sin by whatever circumstances, it is still fair to say that you have saved his or her life. After all, the devil is constantly seeking to devour (swallow up)[19] Christians (1 Peter 5:8), and the heart of the matter in standing firm in recovery against the devil[20] is faith[21] in Christ.

10

Teammates in Biblical Recovery

There are two dangers: Number one, that we (i.e., Christian counselors) will abandon the church. And the second danger is that our field will take over the church.

Dr. Gary Collins
Keynote Address, Atlanta '92

IT MAY APPEAR to some that the above quotation is an exercise in egotistical hyperbole. Yet, as overstated as these words of the veteran professor of counseling at Trinity Evangelical Divinity School may seem to be, they are probably closer to the true state of affairs than most evangelicals, including many leaders, recognize.

A recent feature in *Christianity Today*, entitled "The Therapeutic Revolution,"[1] details the immense clout and status many evangelical counseling professionals now possess and the road that has brought things to the present point. The author, contributing editor Tim Stafford, sees both troubling dangers and hopeful signs for the time ahead. He effectively demonstrates the huge impact of evangelical counseling—especially recov-

ery in most recent years—on the church on the one hand, and
the criticisms leveled at these counselors and their approaches
by many church leaders, most vocally by John MacArthur.
Notable also in the article was the concern expressed by Chuck
Swindoll whose pastorate at the First Evangelical Free Church
of Fullerton, California, included a significant support group
ministry: "There's a lot of schlocky stuff being passed off as
Christian counseling by a lot of schlocky people."[2]

What is not seen in Stafford's otherwise helpful analysis is
a probing of the widespread uneasiness existing between evangelical counseling and the church—not just a few leaders—that
could result in one of the two dangers Collins warned about:
Counseling either abandoning[3] or taking over the church. This
is the missing link in his discussion.

What about the nature of the church and the current
approach to recovery counseling could cause either a full-scale
abandonment or the spiritual equivalent of a hostile takeover
by the counseling contingent? Even more foundational, from
a biblical-theological perspective, does this virtual cold war
have to exist and, if not, how can it be worked through to a
point of understanding that balances the truth in love to which
evangelical believers on both sides of the aisle are committed
(Eph. 4:15)?

In an attempt to address these questions, this chapter will
move through brief pointed discussions of the key New Testament passages, images, and ministry functions of the church.[4]
The related issues, dealing with both recovery and the current
"standoffishness" between counseling and the church,[5] will
be interfaced at the point each naturally dovetails with the
biblical-theological data.

Constructing an Eternally Safe Place

One of the truly helpful concepts emerging from the Recovery Movement is that people in recovery need to be with safe
people in a safe environment. Unfortunately, at the emotional
level, the average evangelical church is often anything but a
safe place.[6] It is, instead, an environment shot through by gos-

sip, judgmentalism, and denial or covering up of deep pain in the name of victorious Christian living. Sometimes truly fascinating explanations, complete with elaborate, out-of-context biblical backing, are given for such behavior. Tragically, though, this behavior is often merely passed on and silently legitimized as normal, even concerned, actions by Christians.

If the church (Gk. *ekklēsia*) that Jesus Christ predicted that he would build in Matthew 16:18 was to be anything, it was intended as a safe place—an *eternally safe* place. Most of the ink spilled over this passage has focused on the identity of the "rock," the meaning of "the gates of Hades," or in verse 19, the nature of "the keys of the kingdom." It is high time that an exegetical-applicational balance be struck.

Since "the gates of Hades," or the power of death (and possibly demonic beings)[7] has no place in the lives of those who are members of Christ's church, then believers are safe beyond the grave. But how do they find safe passage from the point of entry into the church until death?

While it is only realistic to expect suffering along the way (Acts 14:22), it would also seem reasonable for the church to serve as a Spirit-energized safe haven in the storm for those who are suffering as they live in the world. It is virtually the opposite (a fearful spiritual/emotional danger zone) when worldly attitudes and behavior are the rule rather than the exception in the church that bears Christ's name (Gal. 5:19–23). The key point here is that all believers should be able to expect the church of Jesus Christ to be a safe place. This certainly must not exclude those who are desperately hurting because of emotional pain. If anything, healthier Christians need to be willing to "bear one another's burdens, and thus fulfill the law of Christ" (Gal. 6:2).

Support Groups

The only other use of "church" in the Gospels besides Matthew 16:18 is found in Matthew 18:17. This verse is located close to verse 20: "Where two or three have gathered together in My name, there I am in their midst." Some have merged these neighboring words to deduce that "where two or three have gathered" is the smallest and simplest church. However, people gathered isn't by any means the only essential element in a true church,[8] although such a group could possibly qualify as a small group fellowship (Acts 2:46) or ministry of a church. It depends on the group's function and relationship to the wider church body and ministry.

Participation in Christian small groups is certainly a valid biblical option that can fill the individual believer's heart with gladness (Acts 2:46). Yet, if the narrowly focused small group is the only setting in which a Christian is gathering with fellow believers there is a concern. The writer of Hebrews addresses this when he speaks about the need for his disillusioned readers "not forsaking our own assembling together" and hints at what is beginning to take place with his phrase "as is the habit of some" (Heb. 10:25).

Robert Rayburn is correct in stating that "assembling together" here means "the life of the congregation" in general,[9] not just a specialized small group. Certainly it is preferable to participate in a small group than to have no fellowship and interaction with other Christians at all, but this sets up a false choice—either the specialized group or nothing.

This is the kind of choice more and more believers involved in Christian support groups[10] are making. They feel safe, accepted, and understood in the support group, but, after going through recovery, they feel isolated, judged, and rejected in the wider congregational setting, whether in worship or other activities. So they forsake assembling with the wider church body in favor of attending only the support group.

Some who have made this kind of decision have admitted to us that they felt like the specialized group was "my church" or "all I can handle of church right now." Others have expressed hurt or resentment toward the church, such as "I don't care to be involved in playing church with them any more than they care to have me there."

While these are admittedly the true feelings of many who have sought help through the evangelical Recovery Movement but have not found the encouragement they desperately needed in the congregational setting (Heb. 10:25), the church must become a much safer place emotionally because such a decision is, in effect, to abandon the church, and this is never fully justified biblically.

A Biblical Balance

It is one thing for support groups to unwittingly play the role of the wider church in the lives of some of its participants. But responsibility must be accepted when there is active criticism of the church and the directing of group members not to be involved in such unhealthy, judgmental situations.[11] Further, it is quite common to hear about supposedly Christian support groups with essentially no rules or limits except, "Affirm the person" and "Don't interrupt as they vent their pain and bitterness." Frequently, this continues with the same persons stuck at the same bitter points, spewing obscenities week after week, month after month. No one can say anything about the person's attitudes or behavior because it's against the group's rules. Even though these are Christians who supposedly believe that Scripture is the final authority for faith and practice, it effectively doesn't matter what the Bible says.

Surely there is nothing inherently Christian about either of these two points, abandoning the church or abandoning biblical values of conduct. If anything, such outlooks within support groups are as unhealthy, not to mention sinful, as the dysfunctional church ministries they criticize. At best, this kind of approach represents a pendulum-swing reaction: It is no more balanced and probably less stable.

So, what should be done? There needs to be a meeting in the middle between Christians who run support groups and church leaders. There needs to be a practical compromise without a biblical compromise. Support group personnel, who claim to believe strongly in the necessity of accountability, must show themselves willing to be fully accountable to the churches, both by supporting wider church participation and biblical standards of behavior. To refuse to cooperate is to say, in effect,

"We value (at least partly) secular-based recovery counseling/support group methodology over biblical priorities and standards. Go away and leave us alone; this is none of your business."

Church leaders need to be willing to do their part, too. If they expect accountability, they must also be accountable themselves. They must learn what is involved in recovery and decisively lead their congregations in confronting wrong and judgmental attitudes and anything else that would stand in the way of the support of a balanced biblical approach to recovery.

The Key to Biblical Recovery in the Church

The state of leadership in the wider evangelical church today can best be termed "delicate." Without a doubt, the widespread and spotlighted moral defections and divorces of many high-profile pastors and other leaders have hurt the cause of Christ considerably. Thus, anything that can be done to prevent further similar episodes from occurring should be done.[12]

The truly sad part of the present leadership crisis is that hardly anyone outside of need-to-know positions (or a national network/grapevine of friends) knows about half of these incidents. This is not aimed as a cheap shot at Christian leaders, whether vocational or lay. It is simply an honest observation to help cut through the distrustful arm's length outlook such church leaders often take in regard to in-depth counseling as recovery programs.

Christian leaders who do not look at the wrecked lives (and often churches) of a substantial number of their highly gifted former colleagues and say, "There, but for the grace of God, go I," are setting themselves up for a fall. Along with a transparent honesty about human vulnerability should be a willingness to do whatever is possible to avoid the same kind of moral blowout and to model what is learned (Heb. 13:7, 17).

A crucial related point is that many of these incidents were related to recovery issues, which had not been recognized or dealt with before it was too late and the person had hit bottom. While it would be foolhardy to universalize this pattern, it does seem that many highly committed Christian leaders come out of classic recovery-pattern backgrounds.[13]

Ironically, the very leaders who often are unwilling to start the trickle-down effect of acceptance of recovery in the church may well have unresolved recovery issues in their own lives, either deeply buried or unadmitted because of the shame of exhibiting flaws as a leader. Yet, is it not much closer to a life "above reproach" (1 Tim. 3:2) for leaders to admit and deal with the problems than to grit their teeth and stumble forward in shame until those problems get the best of them, their families, and their ministries?

Leaders are the key to the acceptance and employment of a balanced biblical recovery approach. The best way they can show leadership and maturity is to be willing to look closely and honestly at their own lives and family backgrounds,[14] then deal with whatever issues might be found. Any present-tense pain would prove more than worth it because of the lessened likelihood of ministry defection in the times ahead.

The New Testament Models

The New Covenant People of God

Four of the primary New Testament models of the church have implications in regard to recovery. The first two are *retrospective* models, comparing the church to Old Testament entities: the New Covenant people of God and the temple of the Holy Spirit. The last two are *relational* models, reflecting on the closeness possible in the church: the body of Christ and the family of God.

The first model, the people of God under the New Covenant, implies that the church is every bit as much God's covenant people as Old Covenant Israel. Its relationship to the Lord through the New Covenant makes possible a heartfelt reality (Jer. 31:33) and forgiveness (v. 34) not possible under the Old Covenant.

The important thing to ask here is how much is New Covenant newness present in our church? This does not mean new programs, music, or worship forms, although it could be reflected in such things, as much as it relates to the key factors of reality and forgiveness. Both are important recovery concepts. If a church is truly characterized by facing reality and extending forgiveness, its identity as the New Covenant people of God is being worked out in its fellowship and ministry.

The Temple of the Holy Spirit

The second model also looks back—at the temple where sacrifices were given under the Old Covenant. The force of the illustration as used by Paul in 1 Corinthians 3:16–17 is holiness; it also has to do with reality. If someone in the church is merely going through the motions of worship, ministry, etc., it is like the empty sacrificial ritual of the Old Covenant. What the Lord desires from his church is a holy lifestyle based in a realistic assessment of life. Without this reality-based holiness, the church is more like a turtle shell than a New Covenant temple.

The Body of Christ

The third model of Christ's church is the apostle Paul's favorite. He employs it repeatedly to make the point of unity in diversity (Rom. 12; 1 Cor. 12; Eph. 4; Col. 3). The nature of a healthy body is that all of its members are functioning, and all are doing so in unison.

At a motor coordination level, a body whose parts do not work together is considered spastic. At a medical level, a body that has cells at war with each other is cancerous. Being spastic is awkward and embarrassing; being cancerous is deadly.

When the degree of disunity in the body of Christ (the church) is considerable, it is very likely that, from a health standpoint, symptoms of corporate recovery needs should be considered. It would be far better to go through even a painful congregational recovery process than for the body to expire from spiritual and emotional cancer.

The Family of God

The final New Testament model of the church to be considered, and the one closest to standard recovery thinking, is the family of God. This illustration actually emerges from the repeated usage of such terminology as father, children, sons, and brethren. It emphasizes the kind of accepting love (and probably, loyal commitment) that should be present in a healthy family.

Of course, recovery therapy has shown very clearly how families can be breeding grounds for highly dysfunctional and sinful behavior.[15] The same can be true for a spiritual family like a church. But as hard as it is to get a physical family to face its unhealthy patterns (and secret sins), it is geometrically more difficult to get a church family to face the music. But it can be done. Churches that are willing to courageously face the ongoing dysfunctional patterns and stop the cycle of sin will receive a wonderful blessing: They will be freed to be the loving, accepting, committed variety of church families the Lord intended in giving the family model.

A Recovery-Sensitive Pulpit: Preventing, Diagnosing, Healing[16]

A local church that supports recovery (e.g., support groups and referring patients) should also be willing to put its mouth where its money is. No, that was not said backwards. It means that recovery should also be taken into the pulpit and into the educational ministry of the church in a balanced way.[17]

Such a preaching and teaching ministry should not be confused with the typical fare of pop psychology, which focuses on a psychological or counseling concept and throws in an occasional proof-text for the sake of the Bible-oriented hearers. Rather, biblical recovery exposition starts with either a biblical passage, character, or doctrine, then, after making its basic meaning clear, applies it practically to the parallel concepts and issues in the recovery field. This approach maintains the evangelical authority and centrality of Scripture.[18] It also allows the expositor to contextualize theology in a highly relevant, but fully orthodox, manner to the needs in the congregation and of the surrounding society.

There is also the priceless benefit of alerting individuals and families of possible background factors and patterns before they create a major problem. To be *forewarned* may not be to be completely *forearmed,* but it is infinitely better than to find out something *too late.* To even find out later rather than sooner still beats only *getting the message* after the dust of destruction (of a shattered life or family) has settled. At least there is the opportunity for healing and better relationships on the other side of the pain.

Finally, a biblical recovery pulpit ministry offers the opportunity for people to become Christians and begin recovery side by side. Initial salvation is the starting point of the general biblical recovery process.[19] What a blessing if more specific issues rapidly surface and can be worked through early in one's Christian life!

Biblical Recovery Checkpoints[20]

Even the ordinances have recovery connections. Within these, the imagery is of the death of Christ (Luke 22:17–20; Rom. 6:3). When the Lord Jesus died on the cross, he made possible not only bare salvation but also all the various facets that culminate in final recovery. This needs to be remembered and appreciated over and over again.

With baptism, the remembrance and challenge only happens once (although it should probably be implied whenever a believer is present for another's baptism). It should occur soon after one becomes a Christian (Acts 2:40–41), but only after the person understands the meaning of identifying with the Savior's death and resurrection (Rom. 6:3–4), which is pictured in baptism.

The challenge is to live a new life (a recovered life) in the resurrection power of Christ (Rom. 6:4). The grip of the old way of life is broken; it is a complete reorientation (vv. 5–7), very much like recovery.

The Lord's Supper includes the built-in wording, "do this in remembrance of me" (1 Cor. 11:24). These are not painful memories, as in recovery therapy. In spite of the unjustness, Christ's death accomplished the basis of both our salvation and the unity of the body of Christ. It was both the purchase of redemption and recovery and these provide joyful memories, of which a person in recovery can never have too many.

The Biblical Pattern: Supportive Partners in the Gospel

One more aspect of the New Testament pattern of the church crowns this discussion. It is the rich concept of "partnership in the gospel" (Phil. 1:5 NIV) that is the central theme of Philippians.[21] Selfless gospel partnership was the only hope to unify a church ripe for dissension (Phil. 2:2–4). The partnership had been there all along, from the day they had become Christians (Phil. 1:5). But tensions had arisen among those who had previously proven themselves in ministry (Phil. 4:2–3). Some brethren had to step into the breach to restore harmony in the partnership, though it would not be an easy thing to do (Phil. 2:19–30; 4:2–3).

Much the same situation is present in the American evangelical church over questions related to recovery. Those who have been faithful orthodox gospel partners over years of ministry now are in tension with each other. The breach between these church leaders and evangelical counselors cannot easily be healed. But those of us who have stepped into the breach trust that balancing truth and love (Eph. 4:15) will disarm the defensive pride on both sides and reinstate the selfless unity that the world and the church desperately need to see in our day.

11

Biblical Recovery over the Long Haul

Looking back at the power of Christ's resurrection provides the sense of "beginning" a whole new phase of life. Looking ahead to the future resurrection, in which our present limitations and needs . . . will be transformed, we encounter the sense of joyous completion. Then, and only then, will we finally have our act together in the fullest sense. That is the ultimate goal line at the end of the field of spiritual and emotional battle.

Boyd Luter
Looking Back, Moving On

EVERY STORY has to have an ending. Sometimes it is a pleasant conclusion—the rider on the white horse and his rescued damsel in distress live happily ever after. Sometimes it is a very tragic conclusion. Many times the outcome is not known until near the end, but in looking back, you see its connection with the beginning.

154

The story of recovery has an ending that fits this classic pattern. For some, it will be a happy ending as they proceed from recovery to recovered. For others, it will ultimately be a tragic ending as their hard-hearted denial is shattered, and they realize that they have let their opportunity slip by and now it's too late.

A sneak preview of these outcomes of recovery can be seen by surveying the major biblical passages and concepts on the subject of eschatology (i.e., last things).[1] Interestingly, the biblical teaching on last things begins with *first* things. After considering how this overarching passage sets the stage for almost all of the biblical record, we will compare most of the other major aspects of the doctrine of last things to the long-term consequences of recovery.

Finally, a concluding summary of how theology and recovery fit together will be presented, including a chart visualizing the interrelation of the entire system.

Last Things Tied to First Things

The first prophecy of Scripture is also the beginning point of recovery. Victor Hamilton is correct when he notes that Genesis 3:14–19 detail "the consequences of sin" much more than the curses.[2] The first consequence of the original dysfunctional behavior is sin.

In the wake of the first woman falling prey to the subtle lies of the serpent (Gen. 3:1–6), the ironic prophecy is made of an ongoing struggle between the serpent's descendants and the woman's descendants (v. 15). This passage is often called "the protevangelium," meaning the first glimmer of the gospel. But it could as easily be seen as the first glimmer of recovery, since the gospel message and the victory of Christ on the cross lay the foundation for biblical recovery.

When is this passage finally fulfilled? Not until Revelation 20, where "the serpent of old, who is the devil and Satan" (v. 20) is bound temporarily, then permanently thrown into the eternal lake of fire (vv. 3, 10). In between Genesis 3 and Revelation 20, the struggle moves through biblical history, sometimes as obvious as a raging river, other times like an underground stream. This is a very long recovery process, but it also has a very happy ending. In this case, very difficult first things ultimately give way to very decisive last things: The deadly consequences of sin will be no more!

Groaning and Longing for Final Recovery

People with recovery patterns in their backgrounds are not alone in longing to be released from the intense pain of the consequences of sin. The entire created order desires finally to be released from its age-long slavery to the corruption of sin (Rom. 8:19–21). This longing is like the early stages of labor pains before childbirth, only it has continued at a high level of intensity through the entire age since the fall (v. 22). Creation wants the present, painful state of affairs to be ended as much as those in recovery. Even if most people needing recovery are steeped in denial, this seeking of release by nature indicates how closely recovery fits with the prevailing needs of the wider creation.

However, this release will only happen when the children of God are glorified (Rom. 8:17, 18, 21, 30). There will be more groaning and longing before the need for recovery is finally taken away by the Lord. What a marvelous birth this will be: newness beyond recovery![3]

The Deadly Consequences

As we have periodically noted, as freeing as biblical recovery is, many choose to have nothing to do with it. Nor do many of the same people respond positively by faith to the gracious gospel message and become Christians (Eph. 2:8–9). These people gut it out their own way until it is too late.

One of the rare biblical passages that opens a window into the beyond-the-grave consequences of rejecting the Lord and biblical recovery is Luke 16:22–31. Here an unnamed wealthy man who had never given any serious thought to the consequences of his behavior, just his momentary pleasure, dies and goes to "Hades" (Luke 16:19, 23). (Like Jesus' well-known usage of the term in Matthew 16:18, Hades means "the place of punishment of the wicked dead.")[4] The first thing this former rich man learns in his new, neverending torment (Luke 16:23) is that there is a great reversal of fortunes and corresponding role reversal from this life to the afterlife.[5] What he had been before, in terms of societal status and money, meant absolutely nothing beyond this life (v. 25). He had had his chance to change the nature of his life (vv. 19, 29), but by refusing, he had essentially packed his bags for Hades.

People in denial generally do not give either their eternal destiny or possible need for recovery any more direct thought than this rich man. What a shock their eternal abode may turn out to be! Perhaps some of them will sit up and take notice of this testimony of one of their former cronies in spiritual denial before they wake up with a change of address to the wrong side of the tracks for eternity.

The other side of this coin is what happened to a former neighbor of the rich man, named Lazarus, who had suffered greatly during this life (Luke 16:20–21). The fact this man ended up in a heavenly situation eternally (vv. 22, 25) gives real hope to many who are suffering tremendously here and now. It is significant for recovery that verse 25 says that beyond the grave Lazarus is being comforted (Gk. *parakaleō*, a kindred term to *Paraklete*, "Counselor," the name Christ gave to the Holy Spirit in John 14–16). Those who know the Lord and have suffered much in this life will be, like Lazarus, comforted for eternity.

Death—so much a part of the consequences of the first sin (Gen. 2:17; Rom. 5:12)—turns out not to be a terrifying dead end for believers in Jesus Christ. For such overcomers by faith (1 John 5:4–5), death becomes a doorway from their final earthly phase of recovery to the finished status of recovered. When Paul says that "to be absent from the body [is] to be at home with the Lord" (2 Cor. 5:8), he shows no hint of concern or fear about death and reflects this truth.

The final point for biblical recovery in this episode deals with the pivotal role of the written Word (Luke 16:29, 31). People (notably psychologists) can argue about the need for more evi-

dence and research to persuade others to consider the gospel
or full biblical recovery. But when someone who is in a position to know—in this case Father Abraham (vv. 29–31)—
responds to such human logic, the haunting answer is: If they
won't listen to the Scriptures, they certainly won't be persuaded
by other factors (v. 31).

The Ultimate Hope: Christ's Second Coming

It is debated among evangelicals whether the "blessed hope,"
spoken of in Titus 2:13, refers to the second advent of Christ
or the rapture of the church. But it cannot be legitimately disputed that the second coming of the Lord Jesus finally brings
to fruition the *motivation* for both wider Christian living and
specific biblical recovery.

This is clearly seen in Titus 2:11–14. As believers look ahead
to "the appearing of the glory of our great God and Savior,
Christ Jesus" (v. 13), they are also to look back at what he has
already accomplished. Christ has, of course, already appeared
(v. 11),[6] embodying the grace of God (v. 11), as well as divine
truth (John 1:14).

By being able to look back at Jesus' gracious first coming,
Christians can establish a kind of "Point A" in their minds and
emotions. By being able to look ahead to Christ's glorious second coming, they can set up their needed "Point B." And since
it is almost always easier to live purposefully in the present
tense when there is a clear sense of the past and future (i.e.,
moving from Point A to Point B), this is a great advantage in
a world that often seems chaotic and aimless.

Such a past (Titus 2:11, 14a), future (v. 13), and present (vv.
12, 14b) orientation is even more necessary for believers with
recovery issues. They have been ashamed or even traumatized
by the past and are often highly fearful of the future. These
feelings make living in the present a frightening proposition.
Survival is their goal, not living "sensibly, righteously and godly
in the present age" (v. 12).

But those hurting brethren must come to understand with
their minds and hearts that the grace of Christ's first appear-

ing (v. 11) was powerful enough to transform our past, present, and future. Christians have been redeemed from their past, no matter how hideous or far from the Lord it was (v. 14). In God's eyes, they have been purified, that they might eagerly pursue a godly lifestyle (vv. 12, 14). They can do so with the hope that their future, in the presence of the returned Lord Jesus, will be to bask in his glory (v. 13).

Another important angle related to recovery having to do with the second coming is seen in Revelation 19–20. Justice and final judgment will forcefully catch up with both the great abusers (19:20; 20:1–3, 10) and those frozen in denial until the bitter end (19:19, 21; 20:12–15).

Those among us who have been terribly mistreated, or even brutally physically abused, may wonder with the martyrs in Revelation 6:10, "How long, O Lord, holy and true, wilt Thou refrain from judging . . . ?" God's answer to them is also instruction to us: There will be more brutal abuse, even of believers, before the end of the age (v. 11). This is reality, hard and painful though it may be!

But the abuse *will* end . . . forever! When Christ comes again, his decisive victory and rule will focus on completely righteous judgment (Rev. 19:11). Those who have been victimized and brutalized will take part in this righteous judgment and reigning with Christ (20:4).

Since biblical prophecy is history prewritten, we can count on these events taking place in regard to the second coming, we just don't know when it will be. But because they *will* happen, it is fair to call the blessed hope, the "blessed future reality." This blessed future is where you and I are headed, no matter the pain and shame of our past. What greater motivation could there be to move on, full speed ahead, toward the full-recovery future the Lord has in store!

Bodily Resurrection and Biblical Recovery

It should also be observed that the faithful martyrs who reign with Christ do so in resurrected bodies (Rev. 20:4). Eventually, all people will be resurrected (vv. 5, 6, 12, 13), some to "everlasting life," the rest to "everlasting contempt" (Dan. 12:2). Thus, the nature of the resurrected body should be universally important!

Unfortunately, Revelation 20 does not provide much detail about the resurrection bodies that you and I can look forward to. All that passage says is that the resurrected believers are "blessed and holy" (v. 6).[7] But even that is very good news for recovering Christians, whose pasts have often been characterized by cursed, unholy behavior!

Fortunately, in 2 Corinthians 4–5 the apostle Paul has provided additional insight about the resurrection. Having raised the issue of our bodies being raised, even as Jesus' was (4:14), Paul seeks to encourage his readers (who may have been deeply discouraged, even depressed [v. 16]) in the face of visible bodily deterioration and painful affliction (vv. 16–18).

The apostle is here reminding us of the reality that, no matter how good your diet and exercise program (which are important), and no matter how skilled your plastic surgeon (which is incredibly expensive and vain), graying hair (if it isn't dyed) and a gravity-impacted physique are, to some extent, inevitable.

The resurrection body will fix the aging process permanently (1 Cor. 15:42–49)! But it may still be disheartening to some to think that they have to wait until the resurrection for such a renovation.

Happily, the process has already begun! Even as the recovery process goes on daily, the inner renewal process that precedes full bodily resurrection is a daily reality (2 Cor. 4:16). And, if we can see beyond the veneer of our aging bodies, we will observe that the heavy experiences we live through outwardly are "producing for us an eternal weight of glory far beyond all comparison" (v. 17). Such a perspective moves us more and more to the point of longing (5:2) for our resurrected bodies.

But on the other hand, it is also only natural to be fearful of the yet unseen reality of eternal life beyond this life (5:1). This fear is often true even of those who have had ongoing unspeakable horror and pain in their lifetime, simply because the fear of the unknown is greater than what has already been experienced.

What Paul says at that point is an unexpected "zinger" (4:14), but it is a truth that all believers, especially those with recovery backgrounds, need to take to heart! When our mortal bodies die and are resurrected, the difference will be so drastically better that we won't even look back and think of what we have lived through here as worthy of being called "life."

While in this life we must live with the reality of the consequences of tragic acts and patterns, but the time will come when those external and internal scars will be no more. Life as we know it will be swallowed up and replaced by life (5:4) that is fully recovered because it is fully resurrected!

The Rewards of Persisting in Biblical Recovery

The first question many people ask in each new set of circumstances is, "What's in it for me?" For many believers going through recovery, it would be more than enough simply to be released from the painful suffering of this life by reaching the goal of recovery. Yet, that is not anywhere close to all that is in store for them.

The biblical teaching on rewards[8] includes specific promises to: (1) those who remain faithful to the Lord (2 Tim. 4:7–8); (2) all believers who will appear at Christ's judgment seat (2 Cor. 5:10); and (3) those who obey the commands and promises made by the risen Christ to overcomers (Rev. 2–3).

First is the promise of a crown for those who, like Paul, hang in there faithfully until the end of life and "who have loved his appearing" (2 Tim. 4:7–8). This combination of perseverance and hopefulness is honored with "the crown of righteousness" (v. 8). Many pursuing biblical recovery exhibit these traits and can look forward to receiving this crown.

Next is the evaluation of the individual believer's life that will take place before the tribunal[9] (Gk. *bēma*) of God (2 Cor. 5:10). The sense of being recompensed (v. 10) indicates that the Lord will even the score of the inequities in this life. This is joyful news for those with recovery backgrounds, many of whom have been through the wringer, emotionally and otherwise. What a motivation also to godly behavior!

Finally come the "overcomer" passages in Revelation 2–3 and 1 John 5. In Revelation, each of the letters to the churches contains a tailored promise to "the overcoming one" (Gk. *nikao*, from which the English transliteration for the athletic shoe company named "Nike" comes). This term could also be rendered "the victor" or "the winner." Adding the element of faith as the core of overcoming/conquering the world[10] (1 John 5:4–5) results in a lifestyle that correlates with biblical recovery.

The fulfillment of these promises to overcomers lies in the kingdom of the Lord and the eternal state. As with other positive consequences of recovery, these promises take a while to arrive. But when they do, they will be well worth waiting for. What a very rewarding way to live out eternal life!

Eternity: Sinless Newness beyond Recovery[11]

The final setting in which we will consider recovery is the eternal state (Rev. 21–22). There, in a perfect environment far better than that forfeited in the Garden of Eden,[12] recovery overcomers will have the joy of living a fully recovered life forever.[13]

What will such a post-recovery life be like? The first relevant characteristic of the description of the new heaven and earth is *balance*. The dimensions of the city are exactly symmetrical (Rev. 21:16), indicating an overarching sense of balance that will communicate to all who see the city. The second characteristic is *value*. The eternally new city is largely constructed of very precious stones and materials (Rev. 21). Everything, including the inhabitants, is extremely valuable. The third characteristic is *transparency*. For example, the wall (v. 18) and street (v. 21) are completely clear. There is no place to hide, but, without sin there will be no need to hide. The final characteristic of the eternal dwelling is *light*. There is no night (v. 25), and the light comes from the Lord's person (v. 23). There will never be any form of darkness where recovered believers will live forever.

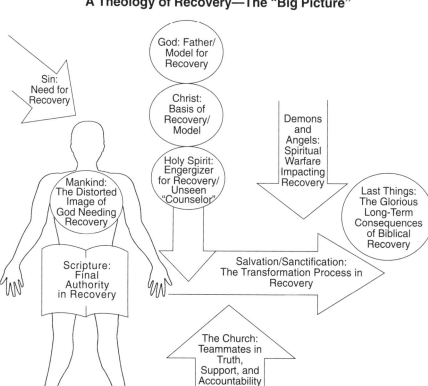

Fig. 11.1

A Theology of Recovery—The "Big Picture"

Together, these four factors not only characterize the eternal life of those now pursuing biblical recovery, they can characterize our lives here and now. We can establish a foothold for balance, a sense of personal value, transparent honesty, and a life of godly light by the way we pursue recovery and our relationship with the Lord of Recovery.

Putting the Pieces Together

All the puzzle pieces of theology and recovery are now on the table and can finally be assembled in their grand design.

The following explanation attempts to balance the contributions of the various parts while still grasping the sense of the harmonious whole.

The authoritative sourcebook for recovery. The foundational piece of the puzzle is Scripture, the final source of authority. All evangelicals must start, end, and stand throughout the process of recovery upon what God's written Word reveals. The contributions of psychology, though helpful in many regards, function like general revelation in comparison to the special revelation of the Bible.

The realistic human need for recovery. The next pieces are humankind, made in the image of God, and sin, which upon entering the human race distorted but did not obliterate the image of God. Psychology and recovery have observed much of how man behaves, including sin, but are not fully able to determine the origin of behavior and its significance.

The divine resources available in recovery. Next comes the relationship mankind has with God. The Father is needed as both a father figure and a model for appropriate parental behavior. While also a model, the Son primarily provides the basis for recovery (i.e., his redemptive work on the cross). The Holy Spirit plays the dual roles of resident (internal) Counselor and the energizer of recovery. Together, the Trinity provides a model and boundaries for harmonious relationships.

The biblical recovery process. The next piece of the picture is salvation (i.e., justification) and sanctification. Actually, it is not possible to relate properly to the members of the Trinity unless a person is justified. Thus, recovery is fairly well limited to God-as-you-understand-him unless the person becomes a Christian.

Along the road to recovery lies the puzzle piece dealing with the realm of demons and angels. Their presence is unseen, but the impact of their warfare dramatically affects the process of recovery. At present, this section is largely undeveloped from a mainstream recovery standpoint.

Nor should the importance of the church be overlooked in the recovery process. If recovery is understood within this kind of a biblical framework, there is good reason to be able to look to the church—or at least some within the church—for needed support and accountability. Almost nothing from the recovery angle, beyond the limited number of church-based support groups, is being done in this area presently.

The end results of recovery. Finally, there is the piece that represents the end of the recovery process. All of the choices that started short term in this life will have consequences for eternity. If someone enters full spiritual recovery and perseveres, the consequences will be glorious. If, however, a person rejects biblical recovery throughout life, the resulting loss will be complete—there will be no further opportunity.

Conclusion

WE COULD NOT legitimately consider this book complete if we did not include a chapter discussing a possible future for the Recovery Movement in the orthodox church. Evangelical recovery is clearly at a crossroads. The question is, Which way will it go? Will it eventually stray from God's Word and introduce further division and strife into the body of Christ? Or will it become increasingly rooted and grounded in biblical truth, bringing God-centered healing to emotionally distraught believers?

We believe the Recovery Movement is in dire need of biblical reformation. While we do not claim to have all the answers, we are suggesting some areas where reform is needed and are offering some possible solutions to the conflicts existing between therapists and theologians. Our fervent prayer is that the Recovery Movement will adhere to the straight and narrow path of scriptural orthodoxy and that the evangelical church will willingly accept and utilize truly biblical recovery concepts.

Theology

There is a need to recover balanced views of certain biblical doctrines beginning with the Bible itself. God's Word is the ultimate authority, and his revealed truth must take precedence over recovery principles, especially when conflict arises between the two teachings. The Bible should not be judged by recovery concepts; rather, recovery precepts should be tested by the Scriptures.

Personal sin, as well as being sinned against, must be acknowledged in the recovery process. It is imperative that recovering believers understand the dynamics of personal sin and how it relates to recovery issues. To face our own sin is to recognize our need for God's forgiveness and mercy. Recovery programs that do not equally emphasize personal sin are not in line with God's Word. In the long run, these programs defeat their own purpose by failing to bring all of God's truth and healing to the body of Christ.

Unfortunately, the Holy Spirit is often conspicuous by his absence in some recovery literature and programs. The Holy Spirit must consistently be invited into the recovery process. He indwells the believer and can see perfectly into the human heart. Therefore, because he knows intimately the broken places of the soul, he can more adequately reveal them and bring healing to those wounded areas.

The Holy Spirit channels his love and support through God's Word and other believers. If he is readily welcomed and acknowledged through prayer, his presence can be felt in the recovery support group and in the counseling setting. Therefore, Christian counselors should actively depend on the Holy Spirit for wisdom and guidance as they work with their clients.

The specific aspects of salvation must have their proper place in recovery thought as well. A Christian is qualitatively different from a non-Christian in many ways, and this fact necessarily impacts the recovery process. A saved person has a new identity in Christ, a new motivation for living, the indwelling Holy Spirit, and a glorious eternal destiny. Therefore, the believer has a hope and a power not available to the unbeliever.

To not emphasize these truths is to again fall short of applying all of God's Word to the recovering believer's situation. Unsaved people who choose to join a Christian recovery group should be welcomed with open arms in the recognition that they are souls in desperate need of Jesus Christ. Hopefully, sensing the Christians' peace in the midst of their struggles, these unbelievers in turn will welcome the Savior with open arms.

Finally, it would be highly beneficial to import the reality of spiritual warfare into the recovery framework. Believers should realize that their unseen foe, the enemy of their souls, will do what he can to thwart their recovery process. More importantly, they should be taught that they have the power, through the Holy Spirit, to resist temptation and to defeat Satan's plan to keep them in spiritual and emotional bondage.

Therapy

Christian therapists and counselors should be more aware of whether a person entering counseling is a Christian. If he or she is a believer, the counselor should emphasize and teach both recovery principles and the biblical doctrines listed above. If the person is not saved, the Christian therapist can address the person's spiritual needs when it is appropriate.

The so-called "Christian" Twelve Step programs must be more precise concerning the nature of God. Any good Muslim, Mormon, or Buddhist could accept the statement "God as you understand him" and thus follow the "Christianized" Twelve Steps. Besides, putting the power of definition into the hands of the people undermines the authority of the Bible, which alone defines the nature of the true God. This is not to say that Christians do not mature in their understanding of God. But it is important that we constantly conform our understanding of God in accordance with what the Bible reveals about him.

Recovery therapists and groups must be very guarded as to how they use the inner child and visualization concepts. While there is some validity to the child within (childlike spirit) and some helpfulness to visualizing past situations, this imagery can easily be carried too far. It can entice people away from God's truth and possibly lure them into New Age philosophy.

It is important not to allow support groups to deteriorate into unchecked, angry, venting groups. Such groups leave the realm of support and become an ideal place for blaming and shaming other people. True biblical recovery and healing cannot take place in an atmosphere of unconstructive criticism and bitterness. Honest feelings should be expressed, but only under the control of the group leader and the Holy Spirit.

Recovery counselors and programs should teach a "Recovery Theology" to believers so they can integrate their treatment into categories and take them into the church to explain their healing process to other Christians. Not only could this benefit fellow believers, it would also begin to help ease the tension between Christian therapy and theology.

Training

Future pastors and psychologists would profit greatly from educational programs that undertake an integration reformation. In other words, Christian psychological training programs should include in their curricula courses that expose the student to integration from a strong theological angle.[1] Rather than beginning with psychological theory and moving to the Scriptures, these particular courses should analyze psychological concepts through the lens of biblical truth. In the same way, seminaries should require pastors in training to take "Theology of Recovery" courses. Pastors and other staff personnel should thoroughly understand recovery concepts and principles so they might adequately minister to the hurting portion of their future congregations.

Professionalism

Christian counselors and therapists must decide if they are primarily servants of the Lord or entrepreneurial professionals. In other words, they must determine if they are counselors who just happen to be Christians or if their faith really dictates their vocational direction and practices.

If Christian counselors choose the latter, then they should be careful not to allow a counseling relationship to go on year after year with no discernible progress. They must be willing to release that client and guide him or her to someone (either a pastor, group, or another counselor) who can further help.

Are Christian psychologists willing to be held accountable to the body of Christ in terms of their theology, therapy practices, and fees? Or will they continue to present themselves as a ministry when it is beneficial to do so, yet be all business the rest of the time?[2] These are some areas counselors should consider when thinking through their relationship with the church and with their clients.

Compassion

Pastors, church leaders, and the Christian populace as a whole must exercise more compassion, grace, and mercy toward believers who suffer with recovery issues. The Christian recovery community has exposed the hard hearts and closed minds of many believers. These unsanctified attitudes have caused much disunity and strife in the body of Christ.

The apostle Paul clearly exhorted us to empathize with one another and carry each other's burdens, thus fulfilling the commandment of Christ.[3] This abundant grace should be poured out on those who suffer emotional distress. If the world could witness this kind of unconditional love toward one another, the church would once again be a powerful influence in our society.

Attitude

Above all, humility should characterize both counselors and church leaders who have been defensive and dogmatic concerning the validity of biblical recovery. The judging and condemning must stop. Both sides should be willing to dialogue about this subject and mutually cooperate to seek a biblically sound common ground.

While there will always be differences of opinion concerning recovery, we must strive for unity between one another. But we must not compromise biblical truth in the process. Recovery is not a passing fad. It's here to stay. We must therefore test recovery concepts by the Scriptures, place biblical boundaries around them, and use these principles to help emotionally wounded believers.

Notes

Introduction

1. Boyd Luter, *Looking Back, Moving On: Applying Biblical Principles of Freedom to Your Life* (Colorado Springs: NavPress, 1993), 18–19.

2. As an exception to the rule, the "Is recovery biblical?" question has been addressed by David Stoop and Stephen Arterburn, eds. *Life Recovery Bible* (Wheaton: Tyndale, 1992).

3. Archibald Hart, cited by Tim Stafford, "The Therapeutic Revolution," *Christianity Today*, 17 May 1993, 26.

4. Ibid., 32.

5. Ibid., 31.

6. Ibid., 32.

7. Though sales of recovery books have declined recently, it is primarily because the book market has been saturated on this subject area. Also, though some recovery programs have dropped in numbers recently, the numerical decline has more to do with increasing restrictions in insurance coverage than waning interest or needs.

8. With few exceptions, the theological categories and viewpoints represent an attempted consensual evangelical perspective.

Chapter 1   The Delicate Balance of Truth and Love

1. The title chosen by Hemfelt, Minirth, and Meier for their primer on codependent relationships, *Love Is a Choice* (Nashville: Thomas Nelson, 1988) describes well the role of love in the recovery framework.

2. The wording "remove your lampstand out of its place" (Rev. 2:5)—based on the explanation that "lampstand" signifies church in verse 20—means closing the church by some unexplained means.

3. Somehow such crusaders are so focused on ferreting out error that they completely overlook the strong gravitational pull of unloving truth toward arrogance. Love must be wedded with truth for true edification to take place (1 Cor. 8:1).

4. If the description in this paragraph sounds like personal insight, it is not mere coincidence. Both of us tended in the direction of such a "head-knowledge" imbalance in our pre-recovery lives.

5. There is no way to be certain precisely what "your first love" means in Rev. 2:4. It most likely centers on love for the Lord as "first priority" or the enthusiastic kind of love you display "at the first" (i.e., in the beginning of your Christian life). But love for other people is closely linked to love for the Lord by Christ in Matt. 22:36–40, and should not be excluded in an understanding of Rev. 2:4.

6. See the discussion of theology proper from a recovery perspective in chapter 3.

7. See the treatment of biblical anthropology in relation to recovery in chapter 6.

8. Though we strongly affirm biblical inerrancy, not all who call themselves "evangelical" do. Thus, the oft-used term "infallibility" has a significantly different meaning for those who hold that the Bible contains errors. But even those with such a viewpoint adhere to Scripture as the "final authority."

9. John Townsend, *Hiding from Love: How to Change the Withdrawal Patterns That Isolate and Imprison You* (Colorado Springs: NavPress, 1991), 77.

10. Ibid., 74.

11. Archibald Hart, *Me, Myself, & I* (Ann Arbor: Vine Publications, 1992), 131.

12. F. F. Bruce, *The Epistle to the Colossians, to Philemon, and to the Ephesians* (New International Commentary on the New Testament; Grand Rapids: Eerdmans, 1984), 333.

13. See the interesting discussion of "Christianity in the Lycus Valley" in Bruce, *Colossians,* 13–17.

14. Though Priscilla and Aquila, Paul's close friends, had returned to Rome (Rom. 16:3–5) at some point since the apostle had been with

them in Acts 18, it appears that their ministry was primarily localized to a house-church (Rom. 16:5).

15. The terminology Paul employs in Ephesians 4:7 (the Greek verb *didōmi* and the noun *dōrea*) are not the standard spiritual gifts vocabulary. However, the mention of "grace" (Gk. *charis*) is closely related because it is a "cousin" word to *charisma* ("gifts of grace"), the apostle's normal way of speaking of spiritual gifts. For a current compact discussion, see A. Boyd Luter, "Grace" in the *Dictionary of Paul and His Letters,* eds. Gerald F. Hawthorne, Ralph P. Martin, and Daniel Reid (Downers Grove: InterVarsity Press, 1993), 372–74.

16. Bruce, *Colossians,* 343–44, has a helpful compact discussion of this issue.

17. Ibid., 347–49.

18. Selected crucial issues having to do with local church ministry and recovery are discussed in chapter 10. Additional issues, including how to preach/teach biblical recovery in a church setting, are dealt with in Boyd Luter, *Looking Back,* 169–74.

Chapter 2   The Authoritative Handbook for Recovery

1. Hart, *Me, Myself, & I,* 10.

2. John Carter and Bruce Narramore, *The Integration of Psychology and Theology* (Grand Rapids: Zondervan, 1979), 93.

3. Hart, *Me, Myself, & I,* 20.

4. See, e.g., the compact survey in Alan Johnson and Robert Webber, *What Christians Believe: A Biblical and Historical Summary* (Grand Rapids: Zondervan, 1989), 36–55.

5. Our quibble with using "Practical Theology" as a seminary department title is that it leaves the unfortunate (and inaccurate) impression that the rest of the departments of the theological encyclopedia—at least the content part of the curriculum—are all "impractical."

6. See the helpful discussion of this theological responsibility in John Jefferson Davis, *Foundations of Evangelical Theology* (Grand Rapids: Baker, 1984), 60–61.

7. The most complete recent evangelical treatment of this subject is Bruce A. Demarest, *General Revelation: Historical Options and Contemporary Issues* (Grand Rapids: Zondervan, 1982).

8. Those who are not familiar with the meaning and sequence of the original Twelve Steps of Alcoholics Anonymous will find a convenient listing in the prefatory material in Stoop and Arterburn, *Life Recovery Bible*, as well as a series of devotionals keyed to the Twelve Steps (see the index on pages 1529–30).

9. Tim Stafford, "The Hidden Gospel of the 12 Steps," *Christianity Today*, July 22, 1991, 14–19.

10. Ibid., 14–16.

11. The new life entered through faith in Jesus Christ (i.e., justification and sanctification) will be discussed in chapter 8 and the work of the Holy Spirit related to full spiritual recovery is discussed in chapter 5.

12. The Greek term is *theopneustos*, which is literally rendered as "God-breathed." See the compact, but helpful, discussion by George W. Knight III, "2 Timothy" in the *Evangelical Commentary on the Bible*, ed. Walter A. Elwell (Grand Rapids: Baker, 1989), 1113.

13. The crucial distinction and relationship between sin and dysfunction is a rapidly emerging theological "Achilles heel" in the evangelical Recovery Movement. It is discussed in chapter 7.

14. W. Bauer, W. F. Arndt, F. W. Gingrich, and F. W. Danker, *A Greek-English Lexicon of the New Testament and Other Early Christian Literature*, s.v. "επανορθωσις" (Chicago: University of Chicago Press, 1979), 283.

15. Bauer, et al., *Lexicon*, s.v. "παιδεια," 603.

16. This topic is treated in depth in chapter 6.

17. Bauer, et al., *Lexicon*, s.v. "κηρυσσω," 431.

18. Bauer, et al., *Lexicon*, s.v. "παρακαλεω," 617.

19. The issue of preaching and recovery will be handled in chapter 10. See also Luter, *Looking Back*, 169–74.

20. The discussion in this section is similar in certain respects to Luter, *Looking Back*, 43–44.

21. Two of the best current resources that provide help with application are Ronald Beers, ed., *Life Application Bible* (Wheaton: Tyndale House, 1988); and Jack Kuhatschek, *Taking the Guesswork Out of Applying the Bible* (Downers Grove: InterVarsity, 1990).

22. For an application of the material in Hebrews to recovery issues, see Stoop and Arterburn, *Life Recovery Bible*, 1379–99.

23. Bauer, et al., *Lexicon*, 237–38.

Chapter 3   The "Father Figure" of Biblical Recovery

1. See A. Boyd Luter, "A Life Worth Living," *Decision*, May 1993, 31–35, for a discussion of the significance of Psalm 139 for issues related to the nature of life and "quality of life" (e.g., abortion and euthanasia).

2. Such a possible understanding is strengthened by the following wording: "And the light around me will be night" (Ps. 139:11), which may mean, "Even in broad daylight, life seems very dark to me."

3. As close to a modern evangelical classic as exists in the realm of theology proper is J. I. Packer, *Knowing God* (Downers Grove: InterVarsity, 1973). A helpful innovative approach to the doctrine of God is found in Gordon Lewis and Bruce Demarest, *Integrative Theology*, Vol. One (Grand Rapids: Zondervan, 1987), 177–335.

4. An excellent, readable recent treatment is Phil Davis, *The Father I Never Knew: Finding the Perfect Parent in God* (Colorado Springs: NavPress, 1991).

5. A compact, yet quite complete, treatment of the divine attributes is Gordon R. Lewis, "God, Attributes of," *Evangelical Dictionary of Theology*, ed. Walter A. Elwell (Grand Rapids: Baker, 1984), 451–59.

6. The factor of balance, as it is needed in the evangelical Recovery Movement, is developed at length in chapter 1.

7. The difficult subject of the divine decree will be applied to recovery issues in the last section of the present chapter.

8. The complementary role of the Holy Spirit in God's adoption of believers is discussed in chapter 5.

9. The next-to-last section of this chapter will apply the tri-unity of God's person to recovery issues.

10. This would seem to be the implication of John MacArthur's viewpoint in *Our Sufficiency in Christ* (Chicago: Moody Press, 1990).

11. See Davis, *The Father I Never Knew*, for an admirable explanation of how God the Father meets the need we all have for a perfect parent.

12. Scott E. McClelland, "Galatians" in *Evangelical Commentary on the Bible*, 1014.

13. See the explanation of the biblical meaning of forgiveness and forgetting in Luter, *Looking Back*, 154–56.

14. Joachim Jeremias, *New Testament Theology* (New York: Charles Scribner's Sons, 1971), 221.

15. Note the helpful application of this verse to recovery in Stoop and Arterburn, *Life Recovery Bible*, 1007.

16. The entire discussion of the Trinity, including a number of practical implications, is most helpful in Lewis and Demarest, *Integrative Theology*, 1:251–88.

17. Problems related to the church and recovery are discussed primarily in chapter 10. The church is shaping up to be the final frontier of biblical recovery, as we realize that it is just as possible for a church family to be unhealthy as a physical family.

18. Among the best treatments of the problem of intimacy offered by recovery writers is John Townsend, *Hiding from Love*.

Chapter 4   The Biblical Basis of Recovery

1. See Rom. 12:3–8; 1 Cor. 12:4–31; Eph. 4:11–13. Many orthodox Christians believe that the spiritual gifts such as healing and prophecy passed away in the first century when the New Testament was completed. It is not within the scope of this book to discuss validity or error of such a belief. However, believers on either side of the spiritual gifts controversy would unanimously agree that Christ is present and working in his church to this day (Eph. 3:14–21; Phil. 1:6; 2:13).

2. B. B. Warfield, *The Person and Work of Christ* (Philadelphia: Presbyterian and Reformed, 1950), 123.

Chapter 5   The Indwelling Counselor in Recovery

1. Hemfelt, Minirth, and Meier, *Love Is a Choice*, 270.

2. The state of affairs may be somewhat different in personal counseling or group therapy sessions, though our interaction with many who are in recovery counseling (and several counselors) indicates that *any* mention of the Holy Spirit is very much the exception, rather than the rule.

3. Archibald Hart, *Me, Myself, & I*, 167.

4. Hart, *Me, Myself, & I*, page 11, also freely admits, "We desperately need a Christian psychology that understands how God works through the Spirit in the innermost parts of the self."

5. Hemfelt, Minirth, and Meier, *Love Is a Choice*, 270.

6. A compact, readable and largely practical explanation of biblical pneumatology is "The Spirit Who is not a Ghost" in Charles Swindoll,

Growing Deep in the Christian Life (Portland: Multnomah Press, 1986), 175–90.

7. Victor P. Hamilton, "Genesis" in *Evangelical Commentary,* 11.

8. The general similarity in imagery between Genesis 1 and Romans 8:18–30 may indicate that the Romans passage is to be taken as referring to a "re-creation" that requires the participation of the Spirit, much as in the creation account in Genesis 1.

9. Other aspects of the relationship between the doctrine of last things and recovery is the subject of chapter 11.

10. Although the phraseology "New Covenant" is not used in Ezekiel 36, as it is in Jeremiah 31:31, the setting of both prophecies during the Babylonian Exile and other parallel features make it extremely likely that both are speaking of the same theological reality.

11. The prophecy of the New Covenant was in effect (i.e., sincerely offered) from the time of Jeremiah and Ezekiel (ca. 600 B.C.) forward, especially when the Jewish remnant returned from Babylon. Apparently, though, it was not put in force until Jesus Christ's blood was shed on the cross (Luke 22:20).

12. Gary Burge, "John" in *Evangelical Commentary,* 871.

13. W. Bauer, et al., *Lexicon,* 249.

14. Biblical salvation (i.e., as popularly used to refer to the theological category of "justification") and sanctification are discussed in chapter 8.

15. Burge, "John," 871.

16. Bauer, et al., *Lexicon,* 137.

17. Burge, "John," 869.

18. Some evangelicals believe that the reference to a baptism of "fire" in Matthew 3:11 is referring to the "tongues as of fire" on Pentecost (Acts 2:3). The majority position is that it refers to a "baptism" of judgment at the end of the age.

19. Though some hold that "baptized into Christ Jesus" and "His death" (Rom. 6:3; Gal. 3:27) refers to the same thing as the baptism of the Spirit, that is by no means certain. One who holds such a view is R. E. O. White, "Baptism of the Spirit," *Evangelical Dictionary,* 221.

20. For further discussion of the body of Christ figure applied to recovery, see chapter 10. For a compact scholarly discussion of the overall concept, see A. Boyd Luter, "Christ, Body of," *Anchor Bible*

Dictionary, ed. David Noel Freedman (New York: Doubleday, 1992) 1:921–23.

21. James A. Davis, "1 Corinthians" in *Evangelical Commentary,* 978.

22. Bauer, et al., *Lexicon,* 109.

23. The favored gift list varies considerably from one sector of evangelicalism to another and even somewhat from church to church in the same denomination or grouping.

24. The questions of the possible cessation of certain gifts, whether it is possible to make an exhaustive listing of the gifts, and what specific spiritual gifts might be on such a list will not be treated here. There is nothing close to an evangelical consensus on such issues and the related argumentation usually does not hold truth and love in its necessary balance for there to be edification (Eph. 4:15). See chapter 1 for further explanation of this crucial balance.

25. Bauer, et al., *Lexicon,* 878–79. See also the related section on grace gifts in A. Boyd Luter, "Grace" in *Dictionary of Paul and His Letters,* eds. G. F. Hawthorne, R. P. Martin, and D. Reid (Downers Grove: InterVarsity Press, 1993), 372–74.

26. McClelland, "Galatians" in *Evangelical Commentary,* 1017.

27. A helpful discussion of the fruit of the Spirit (Gal. 5:22–23) and recovery is found in Stoop and Arterburn, *Life Recovery Bible,* 1308.

Chapter 6   Biblical Self-Image

1. Emil Brunner, *Man In Revolt* (London: Lutterworth Press, 1939), 92. "Man" is being used in its generic sense.

2. See Gen. 9:6 and James 3:9. We discuss the effects of sin on our personhood in detail in the next chapter.

3. See Ps. 139.

4. This may be obvious. But human beings in their fallen state, knowingly or unknowingly, pursue with a vengeance these divine qualities which are out of their reach. We discuss this in detail in the next chapter.

5. For a more in-depth discussion on this view of the image, see Millard J. Erickson, *Christian Theology* (Grand Rapids: Baker, 1983), 495–517.

6. This does not mean that human beings are any less in God's image because they have to grow and mature. For instance, Adam

and Eve were in the image of God even in their state of moral infancy. Their first opportunity for growth came in the garden with the tree of the knowledge of good and evil. For more on this subject see Erich Sauer, *The King of the Earth* (London: Paternoster Press, 1962), 80–83.

7. In saying this, it is clear that God does not grow. He is perfect and infinite. We must grow because we are finite creatures.

8. Original righteousness and holiness were lost in the fall. They are gradually restored to us by reconciliation with God through the process of sanctification. There is more said about this in subsequent chapters.

9. Jurgen Moltmann, *God in Creation: A New Theology of Creation and the Spirit of God* (San Francisco: Harper & Row Publishers, 1984), 220.

10. Hendrikus Berkhof, *Man in Transit* (Wheaton: Key Publishers, 1971), 26.

11. We do not mean to imply that there is never a need for professional help. We simply mean that most people basically need someone who will listen to them and care for them. The body of Christ has been equipped to meet such needs.

12. For a different, but helpful, perspective on the self, see Hart, *Me, Myself, & I.*

13. Some people suffer so desperately with self-hatred that they need professional help. We do not oppose this kind of intervention. But any therapy or counseling that leaves God out of the picture is ultimately destructive because it is not grounded in his truth concerning who we are.

Chapter 7   The Harsh Reality behind Dysfunctional Living

1. Hell (Hades) is an eternal place where people who reject Christ are destined to go. The "hell" here is what we experience in ourselves as a result of sin.

2. It should be understood that the place of alienation we are describing is the condition of a human being before he/she comes to Christ. When a person comes to Christ, he/she is no longer in a state of alienation and no longer suffers the consequences of separation. The person is reconciled to God in Christ. However, this does not mean that Christians cannot fall into sin; it does mean that

they are no longer controlled by the sin principle. There is more on this subject in the next chapter.

3. Karl Menninger, *Whatever Became of Sin?* (New York: Hawthorn, 1973).

4. However, to live with these problems means that our lives do not reflect God's will for us. He does not want us to live in bondage to this kind of emotional tyranny. He gave his Son so that we could be free from darkness and serve him. We discuss this subject in more detail in the next chapter.

5. Romans 1:29–32 and Galatians 5:19–21 clearly delineate such blatant sins against God.

6. William E. Hulme, *Counseling and Theology* (Philadelphia: Fortress Press, 1956), 100–101.

7. This dynamic began to manifest itself in Adam and Eve but is more clearly evident in their descendants throughout the pages of Scripture.

8. The first and second non-empathic environments are being used here to mean environments that are not sympathetic, compassionate, or understanding (i.e. hostile; not conducive to healthy, God-centered growth). These terms are used this way throughout the rest of this chapter and the next.

9. We are indebted to Karen Horney's book, *Neurosis and Human Growth* (New York: Norton, 1950), Dr. Robert L. Saucy (Talbot School of Theology, Biola University), and Dr. John Coe (Rosemead School of Psychology, Biola University) for their profound insights into human nature. We are grateful for the way they have shaped our thinking on this subject and also deepened our understanding of God's Word.

10. For some clearcut examples of mankind's pride and wickedness see Gen. 4:1–10; Gen. 6:1–8; Gen. 11:1–9.

11. See Horney, *Neurosis,* chapter 1. In her complex description of neurosis, she unknowingly epitomizes sinful human nature.

12. We examine salvation and sanctification in the following chapter.

13. See Rom. 3:9–23.

14. See Matt. 6:9–13; Matt. 18:15–35; Eph. 4:25–32; Col. 3:1–17.

15. Even though it is difficult for people who have had a bad relationship with their parents to relate to God, the Bible teaches that

our relationship with him is to be supreme (Mark 12:28–31). See the discussion on this subject in chapter 6.

16. See 2 Corinthians 3–6 where the apostle Paul discusses the transforming power of the gospel in connection with the New Covenant.

Chapter 8   The Process of Biblical Recovery

1. Another passage of Scripture that is consistently used in conjunction with 2 Corinthians 5:17 in order to support the view that the past should no longer affect us is Philippians 3:12–16. For a thorough treatment on a proper interpretation of the Philippian passage see Luter, *Looking Back*, 113–67.

2. For example, see Galatians 5:22–25 and Philippians 2:12–13. These passages do not deal specifically with the past, but they do show clearly that the Spirit is at work in us, producing godly change.

3. "Common grace" means that God bestows his goodness and blessings upon all mankind (Matt. 5:44–45). He providentially cares for his whole creation. But this grace does not save an individual. Common grace does not change a person on the inside. Thus it cannot nullify the bottom line distinction between the believer and unbeliever.

4. See chapter 11.

5. For a helpful discussion on our new identity in Christ see Neil T. Anderson, *Victory over the Darkness: Realizing the Power of Your Identity in Christ* (Ventura: Regal Books, 1990).

6. The family of God, the church, is discussed in detail in chapter 10.

7. It is not within the scope of this book to discuss when the rapture of the church will take place. For an in-depth discussion on this subject see Erickson, *Christian Theology*, 1185–1224.

8. We believe the renewal of all creation will take place after the millennial reign of Christ. Again we refer the reader to Erickson, *Christian Theology*, 1206–16, for a helpful discussion on this topic.

9. Sanctification is used in two ways in the New Testament. It is used to mean either: (1) Believers are set apart (holy) to God (1 Cor. 6:11); or (2) Believers are in the process of being made holy (1 Thess. 4:1–8). This section focuses on the latter meaning of the word.

10. See these Scriptures for commands concerning: prayer (Rom. 12:12; 1 Thess. 5:17); confession (James 5:16; 1 John 1:8–10); repentance (Rev. 2:5, 16; 3:2, 19); obedience (James 1:22; 1 John 2:3).

11. See Phil. 2:12–13; James 1:22; 1 Peter 1:2; 1 Peter 1:14.

12. Obedience also involves following the "one another" passages in the New Testament (see chapter 6). We grow in our relational abilities by being in fellowship with one another.

Chapter 9   The Unseen Conflict

1. This chapter will not directly discuss the origins questions because they are not germane to the relationship between the theology of angels and demons and recovery.

2. Recent examples are Alan Johnson and Robert Webber, *What Christians Believe: A Biblical and Historical Summary* (Grand Rapids: Zondervan, 1989); and the more popular approach of Charles Swindoll, *Growing Deep in the Christian Life.*

3. It should be noted that some charismatic leaders and writers are speaking to such issues, whether from a spiritual warfare or counseling angle. However, a more consensual evangelical approach is seen in Neil Anderson, *Victory Over the Darkness.*

4. Any number of such examples are found in the notes of Stoop and Arterburn, *Life Recovery Bible.*

5. Luter, *Looking Back,* 19.

6. For further discussion of the ramifications of the fall (Gen. 3) for personal sin and recovery, see chapter 7.

7. Though it is not written from either a recovery or spiritual warfare perspective, the comments on Genesis 3–4 by Victor P. Hamilton, "Genesis" in *Evangelical Commentary,* 13–15, are quite perceptive.

8. Though it is not outside the realm of possibility that Job wrote the book that bears his name, most evangelical scholars believe it was written at a later point by an anonymous Jewish writer. If this is the case, Job may never have known what hit him or why. Certainly the prose conclusion to the book (Job 42) does not explain the invisible onslaught to Job, though it does record a striking recovery of sorts.

9. A balanced biblical recovery counseling approach will avoid the evangelical directive counselors' tendency to immediately blame everything on personal, present-tense sin, as well as the opposite angle: the common evangelical recovery tendency to speak of sin

only as that which has been perpetrated toward the recovering person. The second extreme was discussed in chapter 7.

10. To demonstrate how much things have changed in the past decade or so, Carter and Narramore, *The Integration of Psychology and Theology*, 51–52, leave out angelology/demonology and parapsychology from their very careful and thorough subcategorizations of the fields of theology and psychology.

11. Recently, one of us had a conversation with a woman undergoing intensive therapy conducted by a well-known evangelical counseling organization. She had entered the program because of having repeated, spontaneous seizures and surfacing memories of occult ritual abuse, although no physical/medical basis for either had been found through extensive testing. Upon inquiry, she stated that although her diagnosis was still unresolved, there had been no questions or comments of any kind having to do with even the possibility of demonic influence. Obviously, such considerations do not mean that her problems are, in fact, demonic in origin. Still, the fact that skilled Christian counselors do not even seem to be considering this angle in their treatment is more than a small concern.

12. The best formal treatment on the armor and related background issues we know of is Clinton E. Arnold, *Ephesians: Power and Magic*. Originally a scholarly monograph, it has been recently republished in slightly adapted form by Baker Book House.

13. A helpful compact discussion of the armor is found in Richard J. Erickson, "Ephesians" in *Evangelical Commentary*, 1032–33.

14. See chapter 1.

15. The cruciality of the empowering of the Holy Spirit for full spiritual recovery is treated in chapter 5.

16. J. Knox Chamblin, "Matthew" in *Evangelical Commentary*, 738.

17. *Ibid.*

18. This is not at all to say that it is impossible to have assurance of salvation or, at least in many cases, to have sufficient evidence to express whether another person is a Christian. Rather, it is to say that far less than ideal circumstances, like demonization, require a judicious suspending of opinion on the question.

19. Fritz Reinecker, *Linguistic Key to Greek New Testament*, ed. Cleon Rogers, Jr. (Grand Rapids: Zondervan, 1980), 766.

20. Stephen Motyer, "1 Peter" in *Evangelical Commentary*, 1170.

21. See the note on 1 Peter 5:8–9 in Stoop and Arterburn, *Life Application Bible,* 1418.

Chapter 10   Teammates in Biblical Recovery

1. Tim Stafford, "The Therapeutic Revolution," *Christianity Today,* May 17, 1993, 25–32.

2. Swindoll, cited in "The Therapeutic Revolution," 25, 29.

3. The most useful historical antecedent for this faceoff would appear to be the tension between the evangelical church and various parachurch ministries that festered through much of the decade of the 1970s. The similarities are marked, especially the mutual criticism and threats to abandon the institutional church by some parachurch personnel. However, there were no significant claims of doctrinal departure in that dispute and no expressed concerns about secular methodology in sheep's clothing and crass entrepreneurism masquerading as Christian ministries.

4. One of the best introductory evangelical ecclesiology texts is still Robert L. Saucy, *The Church in God's Program* (Chicago: Moody Press, 1972).

5. Some of the theological problems that have resulted in the current rift between evangelical recovery professionals and the evangelical church were previewed briefly in Kathy McReynolds and Boyd Luter, "Recovering through Fully Biblical Recovery," the Viewpoint guest column in the Spring, 1993 issue of the *Christian Research Journal,* 54.

6. Some of the "diagnosis and treatment" of problems in the church in this chapter are similar to Appendix A ("Marks of Safe-Haven and Not-So-Safe Churches") in Luter, *Looking Back,* 169–71.

7. Chamblin, "Matthew" in *Evangelical Commentary on the Bible,* 742.

8. A number of these elements, such as the gospel message and worship, the ordinances (or sacraments, depending on which evangelical tradition you are in), qualified leadership and mission, are discussed, biblically and as they are seen in church history, in Johnson and Webber, *What Christians Believe,* 325–412.

9. Robert S. Rayburn, "Hebrews" in *Evangelical Commentary,* 1144.

10. An interesting point to consider here is that even Christian support groups in churches hardly ever justify their existence from

a biblical-theological standpoint. The methodology comes across for the Twelve Step programs and group counseling. Even if one argued that if something is not prohibited in the Bible it is therefore allowable, it is not responsible to hand those involved a blank check to do whatever they see fit in the supposed vacuum of biblical silence. The gray area activity still must abide by the relevant biblical priorities and standards of behavior.

11. This is definitely happening in some cases, though it is impossible to know how widespread this sentiment is.

12. The noting of these incidents is not intended to cause further pain to those involved. Rather, we would "weep with those who weep" (Rom. 12:15). Yet, it would be a positive outworking of these tragic occurrences if others could learn and grow from observing and understanding what took place.

13. While teaching at Talbot School of Theology, noted speaker and author Neil Anderson extensively surveyed his pastoral ministries students on related issues. He determined that a large number were at risk in the ministry because of their emotional profiles, so he diligently attempted to design ways to help them come to grips with the effects of their backgrounds on their lives, relationships, and ministries.

14. A similar appeal is found in Luter, *Looking Back,* 173.

15. This point is seen dramatically throughout Scripture in Stoop and Arterburn, *Life Recovery Bible.*

16. There may also emerge opportunities for restoring someone who has hit bottom, then repented and worked through an appropriate counseling/accountability period. If so, the preaching in the congregational setting should be a combination of celebration (of the restoration) and warning (not to make the same tragic mistake).

17. Further ideas for expounding biblical recovery are found in Luter, *Looking Back,* Appendix B ("Preaching and Teaching Biblical Recovery: A Basic Checklist"), 173–74.

18. See chapter 2 for a full discussion of the authority of Scripture applied to recovery concepts and the work of recovery counselors.

19. See chapter 8 for discussion of the connection between biblical recovery and the salvation-sanctification process.

20. Because there is no clear evangelical consensus on the mode of baptism or the exact meaning of the elements in the Eucharistic meal, this discussion is general. Standard evangelical Bible diction-

aries or theological resources should be consulted for the arguments supporting the various options, as well as the history of the positions.

21. A. Boyd Luter, "Philippians" in *Evangelical Commentary*, 1035.

Chapter 11   Biblical Recovery over the Long Haul

1. Those who are interested in a more in-depth survey of the biblical and historical development of evangelical eschatology may consult Johnson and Webber, *What Christians Believe*, 415–61.

2. Victor P. Hamilton, "Genesis" in *Evangelical Commentary*, 14.

3. An excellent compact discussion of this "groaning until glory" section (Rom. 8:18–27) is Royce G. Gruenler, "Romans" in *Evangelical Commentary*, 941–42.

4. J. A. Motyer, "Hades" in *Evangelical Dictionary*, 492.

5. Thomas R. Schreiner, "Luke" in *Evangelical Commentary*, 828–29.

6. The Greek words for both the past (Titus 2:11; 3:4) and future (2:13) "appearing" of Christ transliterates into English as "epiphany," a sudden dawning of light into darkness. This terminology is appropriately chosen because Christ brings light into dark and desperate lives.

7. It is significant that the other six "beatitudes" (i.e., blessing statements) found in Revelation (1:3; 14:13; 16:15; 19:9; 22:7, 14) all start with "blessed," while 20:6 begins with "blessed and holy." If so, it would seem that ultimate holiness in a human body comes through the resurrection.

8. See the helpful overview article by Howard Z. Cleveland, "Reward" in *Evangelical Dictionary*, 951–52; and the more specific entry on "Crown" by Peter H. Davids in *Evangelical Dictionary*, 288.

9. Scott E. McClelland, "Judgment Seat" in *Evangelical Dictionary*, 592–93.

10. James B. DeYoung, "1 John" in *Evangelical Commentary*, 1185.

11. The theological issues of the nature of the kingdom of God, the millennium, and the tribulation were not treated in this chapter because there is nothing close to an evangelical consensus in these areas. This is not to imply that they are not important areas for consideration or that there are not recovery-related implications in these areas.

12. The extensive "echoing" of ideas from Genesis 1–2 in Revelation 21–22 clearly indicates that the reader is expected to compare the two sinless environments.

13. See the helpful notes on Revelation 21–22 in Stoop and Arterburn, *Life Recovery Bible.*

Conclusion

1. Institutions such as Rosemead School of Psychology at Biola University do emphasize and teach integration. But the theology of recovery angle should be further developed.

2. Interestingly, virtually the same points regarding the bane of "professionalism" among evangelical counselors are made by Kirk Farnsworth of Wheaton College in *Whole-Hearted Integration* (Grand Rapids: Baker, 1985), 90–91.

3. See Rom. 12:15; Gal. 6:2.

Selected Bibliography

MOST OF THE FOLLOWING WORKS were chosen because of their significance—whether direct or indirect—in regard to the interface between theology and recovery counseling issues or, in the case of publications before recovery came into the spotlight in evangelical circles (ca. 1987–88), psychology. Some volumes were included because of their insight into proper foundational theological content, method, or practical application.

Anderson, Neil T. *Victory Over the Darkness*. Ventura: Regal Books, 1990. This former Talbot School of Theology professor has done a great service to the evangelical community by linking spiritual warfare to counseling issues in a solid biblical and theological manner.

Carter, John, and Bruce Narramore. *The Integration of Psychology and Theology*. Grand Rapids: Zondervan, 1979. Due to its introductory nature, this slender book is sketchy at certain points (which have emerged as crucial in the emerging integration debates). Still, it succinctly maps the terrain and approaches to integration remarkably well and thus has enduring usefulness.

Chamblin, J. Knox. *Paul and the Self*. Grand Rapids: Baker, 1993. This new work from a Reformed New Testament professor develops a fully biblical Pauline psychology of the self, and will, hopefully, stimulate further parallel studies.

Cloud, Henry. *When Your World Makes No Sense*. Nashville: Oliver Nelson, 1990. This book contains many scriptural references, but they are often interpreted through a psychological grid.

Collins, Gary. *The Rebuilding of Psychology: An Integration of Psychology and Christianity.* Wheaton: Tyndale House, 1977. This was an early sincere call for a fully Christian psychology to decisively break from its naturalistic secular "roots," a call which Collins and others have echoed on numerous occasions since.

Davis, John Jefferson. *Foundations of Evangelical Theology.* Grand Rapids: Baker, 1984. The key contribution of this work is its demonstration of the ongoing responsibility for theology to be legitimately "contextualized" to face the issues/needs of each successive generation.

Davis, Phil. *The Father I Never Knew.* Colorado Springs: NavPress, 1992. This highly readable work applies the theological fatherhood of God to the emotional needs of human fathers and children.

Demarest, Bruce, and Gordon Lewis. *Integrative Theology.* 2 vols. Grand Rapids: Zondervan, 1987, 1990. This one-of-kind theological series demonstrates effectively, though selectively, that the task of theology is not complete until the practical questions related to theology have been faced applicationally.

Elwell, Walter, editor. *Evangelical Commentary on the Bible.* Grand Rapids: Baker, 1989. This is a standard trans-evangelical commentary on the entire Bible in a single volume. It is keyed to the popular *New International Version.*

———. *Evangelical Dictionary of Theology.* Grand Rapids: Baker, 1984. This is a standard one-volume theological dictionary. It effectively updates and expands the widely-used *Baker's Dictionary of Theology* (1960).

Erickson, Millard. *Christian Theology.* Grand Rapids: Baker, 1983. This is a standard baptistic theological work for this generation.

Farnsworth, Kirk E. *Whole-Hearted Integration.* Grand Rapids: Baker, 1985. This book presents a helpful analysis of where psychology and theology have both failed in attempts at integration. It is not at all clear, however, that Farnsworth's purported "whole-hearted" method represents more than a "half-hearted" sense of biblical authority.

Hart, Archibald. *Me, Myself, & I.* Ann Arbor: Vine Publications, 1992. This recent attempt at a theology of the self by the respected dean of the Fuller School of Psychology freely admits that even evangelical psychology is deserving of much of the criticism leveled against it from a theological perspective.

Hemfelt, Robert, Frank Minirth, and Paul Meier. *Love Is a Choice: Recovery for Codependent Relationships*. Nashville: Thomas Nelson, 1988. This excellent introduction to codependency only deals with the theological dimension of recovery in a general way but is clear on the gospel.

Hulme, William. *Counseling and Theology*. Philadelphia: Fortress Press, 1956. This is a pioneering work in the field and still has value in current discussions.

Hunt, Dave. *The Seduction of Christianity*. Portland: Harvest House, 1990. The author's contention that evangelical Christianity is being "seduced" by dangerous outside influences includes a "throw the baby out with the bathwater" broadside against evangelical counseling.

Johnson, Alan F., and Robert E. Webber. *What Christians Believe: A Biblical and Historical Summary*. Grand Rapids: Academie, 1989. This unique work does a good job of showing how general evangelical theology developed biblically and has been wrestled through historically.

Journal of Psychology and Theology, 1972–Present. Published by Rosemead School of Psychology, Biola University. This high-quality journal is dedicated to the integration task, though overwhelmingly from the psychological side of the aisle.

Luter, Boyd. *Looking Back, Moving On: Applying Biblical Principles of Freedom to Your Life*. Colorado Springs: NavPress, 1993. This is an exposition of a modified biblical recovery approach, focusing on patterns in the lives of Daniel and Paul.

MacArthur, John, Jr. *Our Sufficiency in Christ*. Chicago: Moody, 1991. The author argues, among other things, that any other approach to problems beyond a directive scriptural one is not in keeping with the concept of the sufficiency of Christ.

MacDonald, Gordon. *Rebuilding Your Broken World*. Nashville: Oliver Nelson, 1988. While this is not technically a recovery book, it is very much a book about recovery as MacDonald shares what he learned through his own fall and painful, but successful, restoration.

McReynolds, Kathy, and Boyd Luter. Viewpoint: "Recovering through Fully Biblical Recovery." *Christian Research Journal*. Spring, 1993. (Reprinted by permission in the Summer, 1993 issue of *Sundoulos*, the Talbot School of Theology Alumni Newsletter.) This brief article was our first published theological critique of the evangelical Recovery Movement and its detractors.

Rhodes, Ron. "Recovering from the Recovery Movement." *Christian Research Journal.* Summer, 1992. This highly critical recent evaluation of the Recovery Movement is not completely even-handed, but it does bring up the common tendency for many evangelicals involved in recovery to almost completely overlook theology in favor of the psychological.

Schuller, Robert. *Self-Esteem: The New Reformation.* Waco: Word Books, 1981. This controversial book was almost universally judged by evangelicals to be non-orthodox theologically. But some of the imbalanced approaches of evangelical recovery leaders today essentially echo Schuller's concepts.

Stafford, Tim. "The Hidden Gospel of the 12 Steps." *Christianity Today,* July 22, 1991, 14–19. This article showed the biblical/Christian "roots" of the Twelve Step programs, roots that need to come out of hiding in some quarters of the evangelical Recovery Movement today.

———. "The Therapeutic Revolution." *Christianity Today,* May 17, 1993, 25–32. The writer chronicles the strengths and weaknesses as well as the genuine contributions and troubling concerns related to contemporary evangelical counseling.

Stoop, David, and Stephen Arterburn. *Life Recovery Bible.* Wheaton: Tyndale House, 1992. This resource clearly demonstrates that the basic concepts in the recovery framework, though not all of its controversial aspects, can be verified biblically.

Stoop, David. *Making Peace with Your Father.* Wheaton: Tyndale House, 1993. This is an excellent explanation and process for working through the pain of estrangement with your physical father, partly by looking to God, the perfect Father.

Swindoll, Chuck. *Growing Deep in the Christian Life.* Portland: Multnomah, 1986. This is a well-communicated presentation of basic evangelical theology with a significant applicational focus.

Townsend, John. *Hiding From Love: How to Change the Withdrawal Patterns that Isolate and Imprison You.* Colorado Springs: NavPress, 1991. This is a primarily psychological work, but one that is heavily biblically documented. His development of the balance needed in truth, love, and grace has points in common with our viewpoint.

Van Cleave, Stephen, Walter Byrd, and Kathy Revell. *Counseling for Alcohol Abuse and Substance Addiction.* Dallas: Word Books, 1987. This book achieves an amazing balance between strong theology and practical readability.

General Index

abandonment, 59, 68
Abraham, 121–22
abuse. *See* sin, sinned against
Adam and Eve, 101, 105, 132–33
adoption, 78, 82–83, 123, 128
Alcoholics Anonymous, 75
angelology, 131–32, 138–39
anger, lingering, 136
application. *See* piercing application
authority issues: Bible as authority, 36–49, 164; love without truth, 26–29

balance, 137, 162; growth and, 33–35; interdependency and, 35; structural, 30; theology/behavioral, 30–32; truth and love, 23–35
baptism, 78, 83, 152
behavior. *See also* piercing application: balanced with theology, 30–32, 43
believer vs. unbeliever, 115–18
Berkhof, Hendrikus, 96
Bible. *See also* biblical recovery: as authority, 36–49, 164; biblical truth, 28; recovery and, 42–44, 135–36; Recovery Movement integrated with, 20; spiritual warfare in, 132–34; theology and, 38–40

Biblical Creed for Christians in Recovery, 128–29
biblical pneumatology, 76
biblical recovery, 35, 113–29, 143–53; consequences of, 155–65; salvation and, 118–19; sanctification and, 125–29; spiritual warfare and, 130–42
biblical self-image. *See* self-image
bonding, 111, 126
boundaries, 15, 93, 111, 126, 137; love without truth, 26–29; theological, 27; Trinity's boundaries to recovery, 61
Brunner, Emil, 89, 91

Cain and Abel, 98–99, 133
calling, 119–20, 128
charismatic movement, 76, 78
Christ. *See* Jesus Christ
Christianity Today, 41, 143
Christian Research Journal, 9
codependency, 15, 93, 110
Collins, Gary, 143
confession, 128
consequence of action, 45
conversion, 78, 120, 128
convicting, 78
corporate choice, 46
corporate growth, 35
corporate preaching, 45
corporate unity, 86

193

Scripture Index

Genesis
1:2—77
1:3—77
1:4—77
1:26—97
1:31—90
2:7—97
2:17—105, 157
3—101, 105, 132, 155
3:1-6—155
3:4-5—132-33
3:5—105
3:7—107
3:10—107
3:10-13—133
3:12-13—107
3:14-19—133, 155
3:15—155
3:22-24—133
4:9-10—133
4:11-15—133
4:16—133
4:17—99
4:20—99
4:21—99
4:22—99
4:25-26—133
6:5—97
9:2—97

11—99
12:12-19—47
20:2-16—47
26:7-11—47

Exodus
20:5—47
20:6—47

Deuteronomy
5:9—47
5:10—47
6:4—60
18:9-13—134
28—48
29:29—48

1 Samuel
6:7—141
28—134
28:3-7—134
28:9—134
28:11—134
28:15—134
28:15-19—134

2 Kings
6:16—138

Job
Book of—133
1-2—133
1:1, 8, 22—133
1:6-12—133
2:1-6—133
4-31—133
4:19—97
32:1—133
42:1-6—133

Psalms
8—97
19:1-6—40
27:10—123
31—95
31:22—95
49:10—97
49:12—97
62:8—94
94:17-19—95
95—46
95:8—46
103:14—97
139—51-52

Proverbs
20:27—97